The House on Nauset Marsh

The House on

HENRY
BUGBEE
KANE

Nauset Marsh

WYMAN RICHARDSON

Illustrations by Henry Bugbee Kane

THE CHATHAM PRESS   OLD GREENWICH, CONNECTICUT

DISTRIBUTED BY THE DEVIN-ADAIR COMPANY, INC.

ISBN 85699-046-9

Library of Congress Catalog Card Number: 55-14552

Manufactured in the United States of America

Contents

The House on Nauset Marsh

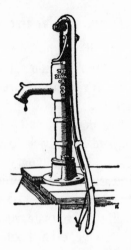

1. The Farm House

YOU can go to Eastham, on outer Cape Cod, and live in the little old Farm House at the drop of a hat. The pump, the kerosene lamps, and the open fire are always ready without fear of frost or storm. You can drive up the lane, stop the car by the kitchen door, and unload your gear. You can look out the south windows over the nearby grassy hills, over the bright blue water of Nauset Marsh to the darker blue glimpses of the sea beyond the dunes, and draw a deep breath.

The morning sun streams through the window of the big bedroom, waking the lazy sleeper at seven or so. This is another example of Nature's tender regard for those who love her. In winter the sun rises at about seven, but it is so far to the south that almost as soon as it mounts over the dunes a mile

or so to the east, it pours its bright light through the bedroom
window. In summer, although rising around five-thirty, it is
ar enough to the north to spare the recumbent form until
seven o'clock as before.

Of course you may dodge, first by edging way over to
the side of the bed, and later, back to the wall. But, likely
as not, a meadow lark will be calling you with a few sweet,
clear notes from a nearby cedar; or a flicker will be beating
a loud tattoo at the peak of the roof. You will probably stretch
luxuriously and sleepily contemplate what the day has in store.
Nothing much, you decide, even should wind and tide per-
mit a paddle down the marsh in the canoe.

At length the thought of bacon, eggs, and coffee drives you
out. An open fire, quickly built in the small living room, soon
provides a pleasant warmth by which to dress. You then step
out and from the south platform scan the marsh for evidence
of fish or birds. You cast a weather eye at the sky, and make
your first guess as to the trend of wind and cloud. Then you
tackle the big stove. If you are lucky and the wind is east, the
coal will take hold quickly. But in a due west wind, the bil-
lowing smoke forces you to abandon ship and to shut the
door between the kitchen and the living room. Left to its
own devices, the fire eventually will start to draw and the
bacon will begin to sizzle.

The kerosene stove is there to use; but breakfast never
tastes the same, the coffee not as rich and smooth, when
cooked over the open flame. Better reserve the oil for early
morning starts or for the warmest summer weather. The
graduated heat and the glow of the coal stove will cook a meal
more to your liking.

A tall man finds that Farm House cooking has its hazards.

The kitchen is low studded and its hand-hewn beams will conk the heads of unwary cooks. What other heads, you wonder, have been bumped by these old beams? The kitchen, in two hundred or more years, must have held many cooks. Our ancestors were not as tall as we of this generation. Perhaps in those early days the occupants had sufficient clearance.

After breakfast you sit and smoke at the oval dining table which occupies one side of the living room—the side where the flying geese are painted on the walls. You sit there in peace looking out through the windows across the hills to the marsh. And thoughts which have long been milling around in your mind begin to take shape. Facts and theories derived from years of outdoor experience and from talks with friends beside a winter fire, or arguments at luncheon in the city, come to the surface of your memory. . . .

2. Gyrfalcon Pays a Visit

ON THE morning of October 4th, 1947, I was sitting at
the dining table writing up the Farm House log, when
gradually a peculiar quality in the calls of some nearby crows
forced its way into my consciousness. Crows can, with their
calls, express almost any shade of meaning. They can be bold,
gossipy, instructive, threatening, warning, or loving—but
afraid, never. This time, however, I gradually realized that
these particular crows were scared, and scared plenty. I went
to the south window and rather casually looked out. Then
I made a grab for my bird glasses, dashed out the north door,
and eased around the southeast corner of the house.

There, above the brown, grass-covered hill which separates the Farm House from the Nauset Marsh, a very large bird came hurtling down out of the air, missed by inches the dark cedar whose top just shows over the brow of the hill, and zoomed up again on spread wings. Then, soaring in tight circles, and with incredible speed, the bird gained a considerable height and repeated the performance. Meanwhile, the crows, evidently huddled in the comforting thickness of the big cedar, gave voice to tremulous croaks of sheer terror.

Although only once before had I seen one, and that but for a brief instant, I immediately recognized this stranger as a gyrfalcon, the largest of all our falcons.

Eight times the falcon repeated his performance, apparently just for the fun of it, as obviously he had no chance to make a kill. Possibly he felt that the crows were getting too brash, and ought to be put in their place. Finally he tired of the sport and headed off to the north, flapping his sharp-pointed wings in a leisurely fashion, but nevertheless making fast time. I had a good chance to observe his generally sooty-brown color, slightly lighter on the belly, with some nearly white feathers near the tip of his tail.

A couple of days later I saw him again. He was flying fairly high towards the dune beach to the east. Again he seemed very leisurely in his flight, and, curiously enough, reminded me of a year-old herring gull. Unlike the herring gull, however, he made the mile and a half from the Salt Pond Creek to the beach in no time.

Next morning, in the fog, while I was sitting on the south platform trying to correlate the obvious follies of man with the feeble attempts of a song sparrow to sing an October song, the big falcon came by, flying low to the south. He suddenly loomed up out of the fog, looking as large as an eagle, and, as suddenly, disappeared into it. He cut through my vague philosophical meanderings, and gave me the feeling that if you really want to do something, you had better go and do it.

The following morning, just as the southwest breeze was beginning to temper the delicious October coolness, he paid the marsh another visit. I first saw him over the boathouses at the mouth of the Salt Pond Creek, where he began to soar. Again, though using wider circles but still with nary a wing-beat, he gained altitude with unbelievable rapidity, meanwhile drifting off the wind to the northeast. I followed him with the glasses until he looked tiny, and became nearly invisible, except where he was crossing white clouds.

Suddenly he went into a dive, came tearing down out of the heavens, and leveled off only a few feet above the tall marsh grass at Pull Devil Corner. From here, he made good time across Tom Doane's Hummock and disappeared somewhere under Skiff Hill. As far as I could make out, he had no live target when he made his pitch.

I have several times watched the gyrfalcon's smaller cousin, the peregrine, or duck hawk, make a similar pitch, usually directed at a single red-backed sandpiper; and I must confess that for speed and quickness of turn the peregrine seems to have the advantage. But when it comes to really magnificent power—power coupled with absolute precision—gyrfalcon has a wide margin over any other bird I have ever seen.

Another two days elapsed before I saw the gyrfalcon again. I had finished that most deplorable of all tasks, locking up the Farm House preparatory to leaving, and was just about to get into my car, when he suddenly passed by not fifty feet over my head. He glanced at me out of one of his fierce dark eyes, but paid little attention to such an insignificant thing, and flew rapidly out of sight to the northwest.

You might think that this was enough excitement for a rather sedentary Temperate Zone dweller, and it certainly seemed so to me. Imagine my delight then, when on April 8 of the following year, I again came upon my powerful acquaintance. On this occasion, a friend and I were on our way to Round Pond. This is a beautiful, absolutely round little pond which in late summer is filled with the scented blossoms of water lilies. It is the most southerly of a group of small "pot-hole" ponds lying to the northeast of the Farm House. Except for the pitch pines, the trees were bare. Consequently, when we came to the locust grove which lies to the east of the back road to North Eastham, a huge bird sitting near the top of one of the trees immediately attracted our attention.

We stopped the car and, with our glasses, looked out at him through the open window. He sat absolutely still, facing us with his head turned slightly to his left. Even at eighty yards, we could make out that fierce glint in his eye. Very foolishly, we elected to get out, so that we might better observe him. Apparently he didn't mind the car, but he did mind us; for, as soon as we appeared, he took off and flew out of sight over a ridge of pines to the east. We did have a chance to see that he was somewhat lighter in color than he was in October. Assuming that he was the same bird, which seems likely, it would appear that the color phases of the gyrfalcons are simply a matter of maturity, as is the case with herring gulls.

The next day, we looked for him among the locust trees; but he was nowhere to be found. Nor did we see him again, anywhere, during that week. I went back to town thinking that our gyrfalcon had left for good. But I was wrong; for son Fred and I, a couple of months later, had the best look at him of all.

It was early in June—the eighth, to be exact—and we were driving back in our open coupé from the vicinity of Round Pond. Suddenly, in the very same locust grove, we came upon him. He was sitting near the top of a large locust, within twenty feet of the road. He was on one side of the tree; and within four feet of him, separated only by the tree trunk, sat a rigidly still and very large crow.

The car traveled another fifty feet before it came to a stop. Then, with the glasses, we took a good look, while from a pitch pine grove a couple of hundred yards away came the excited cawings of a group of nesting crows. It became apparent that the big one was acting as guard for his nesting brethren. I had the impression that he was getting on in years, and imagined that he was an old widower who had taken it upon himself to protect his flock. There was a suggestion of grayness about the base of his bill, which, combined with his unusually long "whiskers," gave him an aged, grizzled appearance.

Like a fool, I made the same mistake I had made before, and got out of the car. The gyrfalcon immediately took off, and the crow, uttering what can only be described as a loud squeal, took off after him. I am sure it was a warning signal; for those more distant crows at once fell silent. We observed that the gyrfalcon now had so many white feathers on his wings and back as to appear distinctly mottled. Then both birds disappeared over a rise to the east. I have not seen him since.

As the days roll by, in my mind I can see this magnificent

bird sitting bolt upright on the top of a rock, ranging the arctic tundra with his glowing eye. I like to think he will again take up traveling. If he does, I am sure the memory of those rolling downs, of that exquisite, open-water Nauset Marsh, of the wide ocean, whose deep blue color defies description—I am sure the memory of all this will sometime bring him back.

3. Direction Sense

HOW do birds, animals, and even fishes find their way about? This intriguing problem has interested many naturalists. I have never heard of any adequate explanation, and herewith offer my own, which is pure theory.

Many birds migrate long distances. Yet banding operations seem to indicate that they do not often get lost; for year after year the same bird will return to the same station. If he does not return, the chances are all in favor of the bird's having met with violent death.

I remember, late one September, watching the antics of a "winter" (greater) yellowlegs. It was one of those beautiful, rather still, crisp, clear days not infrequently seen at this time of year on outer Cape Cod. The sun was getting high, and large, puffy, white cumulus clouds were forming. The yellowlegs started to fly in wide circles over our hill. After reaching an altitude of about three hundred feet, he set his wings and began to soar. I never had seen a yellowlegs do this before, and never have since. Soaring in circles, with no wing motion, he rapidly gained height, rising almost as rapidly as would that monarch of the air, the duck hawk. Soon the bird was invisible against the deep blue of the sky, but he would reappear as he circled under a big white cloud. Finally, a tiny speck, he straightened out, and took a course slightly to the west of southwest, and disappeared into the blue.

Did he gain such height in order to get his bearings? Or did he do so to take advantage of favorable upper air currents?

If birds follow their migration routes by picking up landmarks, it is obvious that the young of the year must be shown the way. There is some evidence that Canada geese do actually follow landmarks, and that the elders of the family, or of several families, take their children with them, presumably to teach the way. The familiar "V" of flying geese is always, at least when it can be determined, headed by an old bird. Incidentally, this formation appears to be the most efficient, but throws considerable burden on the leader. I have observed and others have commented on the changing of leaders, which undoubtedly occurs often during a migration flight. When a thick fog unexpectedly descends (and I use the word "unexpectedly" because Canada geese seem to be quite choosy about what weather they fly in), not infrequently a flock of geese will become obviously lost, take three turns around the Congregational Church, inspect the few commuters on the five-fifteen, and finally light and spend the night in the ball park.

In the spring, migrating Canada geese, when they pass the Nauset Coast Guard Station, are taking a course that is almost exactly east-northeast, magnetic. However, when they reach the region of the Gaspé Peninsula and the island of Anticosti, they suddenly, at about the same spot, I am told,

HENRY
BUGBEE
KANE

make a right angle and fly to the northwest. Thus they come to their usual breeding grounds north and east of Hudson Bay, along Hudson Strait, and across it to the south coast of Baffin Island.

These observations tend to suggest that Canada geese on long flights make considerable use of previously learned landmarks. I believe, however, that this is rather unusual with most birds.

For instance, the great flights of black-bellied plover seen on the outer Cape are headed by adults, those smartly dressed, black-fronted and white-browed owners of the August sand flats. Later on, in September, come the youngsters, the "pale-bellies," often in large numbers. At this time, "black-breasters" are few and far between. One could, of course, assume that an army of immature plovers is led by one or two adults, the whole kept in company by constant calling back and forth. There is no doubt about the fact that individuals in migrating flocks maintain a liaison by constant calling, as anyone who has slept under the stars during active migration can attest. However, the disproportion between the numbers of immature pale-bellies and their black-fronted elders is too great to make this theory attractive. It seems to me almost certain that these newly feathered birds find their own way down the coast.

I have no significant data in regard to the black-breaster's cousin, the golden plover. On the east Atlantic coast, these birds take off from the region of Nova Scotia and fly oversea to South America. There is little evidence that they stop on any intervening islands, although reports of their resting on the bosom of the sea have been recorded. If the golden plover follows the same rule as its close relative, the birds of the year should end up the flight in large numbers, and these flights should include few or no adults. In any case, how do these large flocks fly true to Argentina and Brazil?

Then what about those ocean wanderers like the fulmars and the shearwaters? Do they know where they are? Incidentally, at least some of the shearwaters reverse the "normal," by doing what almost anyone would have expected. That is, they nest in the southern hemisphere during our northern winter, and migrate north when temperate northern zones are enjoying summer. It is astonishing how few birds do this.

The Manx shearwater is an exception, however, and, during our summer, nests in Wales. Of two brooding birds which were removed from their nests and released in Venice, one returned to its nesting site in fourteen days, but the other waited until a year later. It has been implied that the slow bird refutes the evidence of the fast one. To me, the amazing thing is that both of them returned to their native Wales.

Ornithologists have long speculated about the possibility of oceanic birds using trade wind swells to direct their course. F. W. Preston in "The Auk" (*General Notes*, January 1949) has offered what is to me a new suggestion in this regard. He points out that, at certain seasons, specialized cloud formations may develop and remain constant over specific ocean currents. Such clouds, or fog banks, could be used by birds as easily as mountains, coasts, or rivers. This theory also brings to mind the possibility that oceanic birds might be guided by the color of the water. The difference in color between the Gulf Stream and the Labrador Current is obvious to all mariners; and there must be many other areas where thick plankton might offer more or less constant color differentiation.

Some years ago, noddy and sooty terns were taken from their nests on the Florida Keys, banded, and put aboard east-bound ships. They were liberated after several days at distances up to eight hundred and fifty miles, and most of them returned to their nests.

More recently, a study of Leach's petrels was made by Alfred O. Gross and his associates. These fork-tailed petrels —possibly "Mother Carey's Chickens" to you—make their burrowed nests in the cliffs of the region of the Bay of Fundy. Brooding petrels were captured, banded, taken across the peninsula, and liberated. Some were also put in holds of freighters, placed on phonograph disks so that they were constantly rotated, and then set free. I do not remember the exact distances traveled, but they were in the neighborhood of 400 to 800 miles. This distance was limited by the fact that there was no way to keep the birds alive.

Anyone who has observed the dainty ballet of the feeding petrel, as it pirouettes lightly over the surface of the water with outstretched feet, must realize that it will not accept a diet of Wheaties and peanut butter. However, the distances achieved were considerable, and a very high percentage of the birds returned to their burrows. Some of the nearer birds took their time, and of the further birds some arrived home in a few days, while others took two weeks or so. Nevertheless, the fact remains that most of the birds returned.

Now what about animals? There are innumerable stories about dogs finding their way home. One I remember is that of the well-beloved family setter who had to be sold and was taken about 450 miles, mostly in a baggage car but partly by automobile, into strange country. Three weeks later—dirty, ragged and thin—he was back at home. Such homecomings, from varying distances and under varying conditions, have been reported over and over again.

As to fishes, it is quite possible that there is an orderly migration of such fish as the cod, haddock, striped bass, and mackerel. I am particularly intrigued with the eels. As I understand it, the North American Atlantic eels leave the rivers, head for the Sargasso Sea, and there (or not far from there) lay their eggs. The European Atlantic eels do the same thing, leaving something like a 300-mile gap for the sake of privacy. When the eggs hatch, the larvae immediately start for their respective shores, which they reach in two years or so.

This is all the more remarkable since the American eels, especially those headed for north of Cape Cod, need to leave the friendly Gulf Stream and struggle up against the Labrador Current. On the other hand, the European eels must have to swim in circles, in order not to reach their home river too soon; that is to say, before they have grown to the elver stage where they have assumed the adult eel shape. However this may be, how does this tiny baby eel find its way back to continental shores? Unlike the salmon, there is as yet no evidence that the eel returns to its parent stream.

It is well known, of course, that the Atlantic salmon returns to the stream in which it was born. What the salmon does with its time off is still a matter for considerable speculation; and how it finds its way back has not been explained. Some think the salmon remains at great depths in the ocean, but still within the sunken valley of its own river.

The question is, then, how do these birds, animals, and fishes find their way about?

I believe that these creatures have a definite "direction

center" in their brains. I suspect that this center is very sensitive to some one of the known, or perhaps unknown, forces which are continually bombarding the earth. It does not seem to me impossible to believe that these centers can pick up the electromagnetic forces which cause a magnetized needle to point toward the north. In other words, I believe birds, animals, and perhaps fishes have, in fact, a protoplasmic, biological compass. Man has evolved beyond the necessity for such apparatus, and so has lost it, as he has lost to a great extent his sense of smell and touch. Consequently, man must carry a compass, conceived and made by his brain and hands, if he wishes to preserve his life when the tide floods the flats just as a thick fog shuts in. Such a theory might in part explain the alleged confusion of the homing pigeon when approaching high-powered radio stations.

I thought these ideas were original, but, as often happens, I have since found out that many others have been thinking along the same lines. In the September, 1947, issue of *Life*, H. L. Yeagley suggests that birds in some way can sense the rotational force of the earth ("Coriolis force") as well as the magnetic force. He made a chart showing where these two lines of force would cross at the same angle and with the same intensity as at his dovecot in Pennsylvania. Such a situation occurred in Kearney, Nebraska; and he promptly took out a batch of homing pigeons and released them without giving them the opportunity to learn the terrain. He obtained a reasonably high percentage of returns, which he considered significant. He further claimed that if you tied weak magnets to the wings of homing pigeons, they did badly compared to birds flying with unfettered controls. Others, though willing to concede that, mathematically speaking, the results were somewhat outside the range of pure chance, seem inclined to discount both the theory and the reported observations.

D. R. Griffin has followed, by airplane, gannets which were taken from their nests on Bonaventure Island in the Gulf of the St. Lawrence and released, presumably in unfamiliar territory, over northern Maine. The gannets followed a most erratic course, flying hither and yon with no apparent purpose. This description reminds me of ants which I have watched as they worked their way back to their burrows. Griffin concludes that these gannets were simply looking around for landmarks. One could, however, take the point of view that they were trying to "bracket" a weak magnetic or other signal from some fixed point—that, in other words, they were "coursing" to get the "scent" from some source which would guide them home. Also, it seems to me that he fails to explain what good this erratic flight of the gannets, in unfamiliar territory, could have done them. The extraordinary thing is that they all did return to their breeding island.

Whatever the answer to all this may be, let no one underestimate the power of nerve tissue, whether in man or fish. Man's thoughts are accompanied by electrical discharges which can be measured. The force of these discharges seems picayune indeed when compared to that generated by some fishes. This is perhaps a wise provision of nature, when one considers that the electrical discharges from these fishes can knock a man down, or even, it is said, kill him.

Is it, then, too fantastic to believe that these "lower" animals actually have a direction center in their brains, by means of which they find their way about?

4. *Are Birds and Animals Intelligent?*

WHENEVER I venture the suggestion that either bird or animal has acted intelligently, my scientific friends begin to hoot. Only man can show signs of intelligence, they say; to which I reply that man seems easily able to hide this fact. "What is intelligence?" I ask. The answer sometimes given is that intelligence means the power to reason, which involves the use of memory and the ability to count. Birds and animals cannot count, at least not much; they have little memory, and therefore cannot reason.

One winter Sunday, many years ago, when I was stationed at Camp Devens, I went for a walk through an eight-inch fall of light snow. Suddenly a deer jumped up, not thirty yards off, and bounded away in great leaps, until his flashing tail disappeared behind a windfall. This was the last I saw of him, in spite of the fact that he was my companion for most of the day. I followed his tracks into a swampy wood. He discovered that I was following him and made a circle about a quarter mile in diameter. I went around it twice before I found the spot where he jumped out. Again we took a loop and came back to the same circle, which he then crisscrossed several times. And again I followed him out. This happened three times. Finally he tried a new tactic and went straight away for five or six miles. Eventually, however, we started to turn. I found some hair on a barbed-wire fence that he had jumped, and wondered which of us was the more tired. We turned more and more, and sure enough, another six miles and we were back in the original maze. By this time I had so tramped down the area, and the light was becoming so poor, that I could not find exit tracks. I gave up the chase, dog tired and full of admiration for the beast's intelligence.

"That wasn't intelligence," said my scientific friend.

"What was it?" I asked.

"Instinct," he replied.

Try sometime to get a clear definition of instinct. Most people know in a general way what it means, but I have never found anyone who could tell me what it actually is.

Well, maybe the deer was just responding to experience previously gained; perhaps, in other words, he had developed a "conditioned reflex." This is the term which is used by scientists to account for animal intelligence. In this instance there was no reasoning involved, they would say; otherwise the deer would have known that I was depending on sight and not on smell, and would have abandoned his maze. However, as it turned out, this might have been a very foolish thing to do. Besides, I am not saying that a deer has human intelligence; he may have something better—at least better for a deer.

The setting sun was just about to touch the brow of Skiff Hill. Suddenly my spine tingled as the honking of distant geese came down from the sky. Soon they flew overhead, high, from the north, about twelve of them, their white breasts reflecting a golden sheen. The old gander was in the lead as the geese circled the marsh once, all of them talking and gabbling, trying to decide whether to stop or to fly on south. Then a sterner note crept in; the other honkers became silent, and the old gander gave his orders. The flock continued to circle slowly, at six hundred feet; but the gander came down to about one hundred feet and swung around the entire marsh. Finally he found a place he liked and called again. The whole flock suddenly broke ranks and came side-slipping and zigzagging out of the air, with a roar of wings. At the last moment, they came together and gracefully settled down on the Beach Marsh.

How then describe the behavior of this venerable bird which showed all the qualities of leadership, involving a cautious weighing of risks, great courage, and absolute unselfishness? Was this instinct? Or a combination of previously conditioned reflexes? Call it that if you will; you are simply quibbling over terminology.

"Fatty Spilliker" was a very large foxhound. His largeness was due to fat, as his name—which some old-time comic strip readers may remember—implies. Consequently, he was extraordinarily slow on his feet; but he had a wonderful nose and great tenacity. I can remember one time when he stuck to a trail for two nights and one day. When he finally came back to camp, he was close to a state of exhaustion shock.

Anyhow, Fatty Spilliker started a fox in Fulcher's Swamp, and could be heard baying away at a great rate. Finally his owner took a gun and hid himself behind an old, tumble-down shack that overlooked the swamp. Pretty soon, at the edge of the bushes, old Fatty came lumbering along, every once in a while giving forth with his peculiarly melancholic wail. And about thirty feet behind him came the fox, who had lapped Fatty and was now close behind him. Round and round they went, until Mr. Fox tired of his sport and raced off across the hills to the railroad track, where, I have no doubt, he ran down a rail for several hundred yards. Fatty's owner could have killed the fox and secured his pelt, but he had no heart for it, and went home chuckling.

Here we have an animal showing not only intelligence but a sense of humor. This is important because some people insist that a sense of humor is an integral part of human intelligence. I have never heard a fox laugh, but I am willing to bet that this fox had a good laugh at Fatty's expense when later he safely returned to his burrow beside the crooked cedar.

"Flash" was a chestnut-colored Chesapeake Bay retriever, somewhat along in years. He was an extremely "intelligent" dog, who did his work diligently and without mistake, never getting himself into trouble, and saving for the camp large numbers of ducks that otherwise would have been lost. He never went out on ice too thin to hold him; nor did he allow himself, while swimming after a wing-broken but otherwise healthy duck, to become so exhausted that a boat expedition was required to save his life.

Some may not agree, but I always thought he showed considerable wisdom in the following incident. He and his uncle, "Bright," had been waiting around hungry for hours, while the crew at the camp had been eating dinner. At this particular meal my father, who had a peculiar passion for tripe, had tried to make his family eat and appreciate it. Unfortunately, nobody shared his views, and a large platter of tripe was returned to the kitchen. John, who helped us run the place, took the platter and dumped the contents into the dogs' pans as they crowded around with mouths drooling. They made a simultaneous leap for their dinner, took one sniff, and then slunk off around the corner of the house, their tails between their legs.

My father decided we had better start training a puppy. One day, much to Flash's surprise, a boxed cage with a three-months-old puppy in it was put down on the gun-room floor. Flash came up suspiciously, took a look and a sniff, then lifted his leg and thus expressed utter contempt. Some might consider this action the first sign of jealousy; but Flash's judgment proved sound. The little puppy, "Jake," though he grew up to be a lovable cuss, turned out to be the darndest fool dog there ever was.

Among birds, the wily black duck certainly has a deserved reputation for seeming intelligent. Anyone who has spent long hours lying half-frozen, flat on his back, with blackened face and camouflaged boat, waiting for ducks to come within forty yards of him, will swear to this bird's intelligence. The high-flying old devils will circle and circle, each time setting their wings as if they were coming right in, and then they will flare just out of range as they see something not quite to their liking. They will light in mid-channel, swim up to within one hundred yards of the set and back down again, finally working into the sedge at a safe point well away from harm. What if they have once been shot at? The intelligent thing to do, if you have been shot at from a set of duck decoys, is to avoid the trap the next time.

Crows, aside from an apparent individual intelligence, have a very well organized society. I agree with the late Ernest Thompson Seton that they have a rather elaborate "language." Often, in the early morning, I have watched them gather on the roof of my brother's house and talk over the day's plans. During this time, they are in touch, by voice, with distant scouts. Finally the caucus is ended, and they will straggle off to an appointed destination. At all times, however, they appear to be in communication with the entire crow population, by means of deliberately placed liaison units; for let a big owl or a fox appear, and in no time a hundred crows will be badgering him.

There are many stories about tame crows, but I like best the one my cousin tells. His crow enjoyed sitting on the top of the archery target while they were practicing the York round—say at eighty yards. An arrow would come whizzing into the red, plunk! The crow would simply turn his eye. He would cock his head again and watch an arrow thump into the gold. Next time, he would lightly jump up a scant six inches and let the arrow pass under him, or duck slightly and let the arrow pass over. He never appeared to become nervously upset by the hazards of this sport, accepting them with the nonchalance of the true gambler.

I have written this chapter with tongue partly in cheek. As a scientist myself, I know how easy it is to hide one's ignorance by using long words and high-sounding phrases. Perhaps birds and animals are more intelligent than man thinks —and man less so.

5. *Time Sense*

AS I understand it, mathematical formulas, except perhaps for one, cannot determine whether time is going forward or back. These laws are exactly as applicable from present to past as they are from past to present, or, for that matter, from present to future. The one exception has been described as the "scattering tendency." This term, to me, means simply that things happen, upon which depend the happenings of other things. Because of this, one can be certain that time is moving forward.

I have been interested in noting my own sense of time. No matter how deeply I sleep, when I awake I know that time has passed. In fact, when "in training" I can awake at any required hour without the help of an alarm. When really in practice I can count on hitting the time within ten minutes either way. Even now, when I have to do it, I can, upon waking unexpectedly, usually guess the time within half an hour either way.

What is the mechanism of this peculiar ability which we all have to a greater or less extent? It must have a physiological basis; if so, it must mean that a cerebral center has the job of recording some type of chemical reaction—a reaction which is not reversible—and transposing that reaction into a consciousness of clock time. Such a center is probably closely related to a similar center which has to do with some feeling of direction.

During the first World War, in the year 1918, I had many occasions to use this already developed faculty. I could, after twenty-four hours without sleep, drop into a sound slumber and wake up two hours later in order to check up on previously arranged outposts. In more peaceful surroundings I could wake up in time to set out decoys a half hour before sunrise. However, when out of practice, one's sleep may be interrupted, and frequent inspections of the clock may result.

There is much evidence that slumber is deepest during the first three or four hours. Experiments involving the height from which a constant weight must be dropped in order to awaken a sleeper have shown that the heavy sleep curve occupies the first two to four hours, following which there is a sharp descent to near-waking levels again followed by a secondary rise. (The latter comes just when it is time to get up and build the fires.) Even so, one can learn to wake up at any time during the cycle.

The effect of complete ether anesthesia is further evidence that there is a time center. During such anesthesia one loses all sense of the passage of time. The last conscious observation is immediately tied to the first waking one, and the feeling of surprise that it is "all over" is very commonly spoken of. Ether anesthesia obliterates the time sense, as it does all higher cerebral activities.

On the other hand, morphine, dilaudid, and codein do somewhat the opposite. The effect of these drugs is to slow the clock. One will sleep under the influence of dilaudid, say, for what seems like hours, only to awaken and find but twenty minutes of elapsed time. Curiously enough, the effect during wakefulness is the opposite. When one is awake all these drugs seem greatly to hurry the passage of time. This is in part due to relief of pain and the causing of a slight euphoria; nevertheless, I think the effect is more profound than can be explained on this basis alone.

It is, of course, common observation that if one's day is filled with doings, time seems to be passing rapidly, whereas in retrospect it appears to have passed slowly. The reverse is also true; if one is bored, time appears to pass slowly, while in retrospect it seems to have passed rapidly.

Finally, time, as far as any individual is concerned, appears to go faster and faster the older one gets to be. This would seem to be a wise provision of nature which thus cushions what might become the boredom of old age.

I have often wondered if birds also have a time sense. Certainly it seems as if the herring gulls could time the tide very closely. We see them lazily gliding across the Cape, arriving at our marsh just as the water over the flats shoals enough for them to reach bottom. The black-bellied plover arrive commonly at dead low water; but this may be simply because

they are lifted off the West Shore flats, low water in the Nauset Marsh occurring two or three hours later than on the West Shore. But how account for the herring gulls who have spent the high water washing up in the Great Pond? Or the greater yellowlegs who seem to know so well when the tide will be low enough for them to chase minnows on the flats, having slept while the tide was high on the north shore of the same Great Pond? Surely these birds have some sort of time signal clicking off the minutes, even though they are not "conscious" of it.

On the other hand, the birds became really bewildered during the total eclipse of the sun on August 31st, 1932. As I remember it, totality occurred about four o'clock in the afternoon. When sudden twilight shut down over the marsh the terns gathered in large flocks as they do at sundown, circled to gain height, and started off to the west toward their nightly roosts. They could hardly have crossed the Cape before the abruptly released sun again flooded our world with dazzling light. Unfortunately, in the bustle and excitement of the moment (there were thirty-three members of the Richardson clan sitting on the hill in front of the Farm House), I did not notice whether the terns came back.

It is my belief, then, that there is a "time center" located somewhere in the brain of man, and very probably in that of mammals, birds, and possibly even in fishes. In man, this center can be "harnessed," with some practice. Yet it is doubtful if man will ever equal his feathered friends in making a punctual appearance at the dinner table.

6. *Roccus Lineatus*

MY FATHER claimed that he fished for striped bass in the Weweantic River for twenty-five years before he caught one. This story I am sure lost nothing by repetition, and there are no details as to how often he fished the Weweantic. However, it is true that for several years before he died in 1912, we began to catch a few nice bass in the river. Great fisherman that my father was, no catch gave him greater pleasure than a Weweantic striper.

We used to fish at low water, out of a sailing skiff, with trolling rods. Mel Marble would string a small eel with a tandem of two or three hooks, and fit a small, conical sinker over the nose. We caught all our fish in the mile stretch above the wharf up to the high tension wires below the bridge. We never caught more than three on a single trip; and many, many times we came home without any. (I might add that I still do.) However, I did make a record I have never seen duplicated. I caught two striped bass at the same time! We were sailing with a fresh sou'wester on the quarter, when I struck a good fish. Mel luffed up and let the sheet go. After a brisk fight I thought the fish was coming in, when he seemed to take on a new lease of life, and it took another five minutes to bring him up to the boat. Imagine our surprise, when through the brown water we saw two fish, one on the upper and one on the tail hook. Mel somehow got them both into the net and landed them. They were not large, five and two pounds as I remember it, but I was the proudest boy there ever was.

I began to haunt the Nauset Marsh in 1912. In 1924, my brother Edward arrived at the Farm House with a lemon-wood rod and a reel equipped with a clutch and a free-running spool. His thought was that striped bass were coming back, and why shouldn't we have some fun with them, much as they did on the Jersey beaches. Up to that time, a few bass were being caught off the beach by "heavers and haulers," especially in the fall. The only early Farm House record for bass appears in the 1921 log. On this occasion, while shore bird shooting, we noticed large fish breaking water in the channel. The next day we trolled from a canoe, with trolling rods and a mackerel jig covered with a large whitebait. We caught three bass, weighing one and a half, two, and three pounds. We did a lot more fishing in this and subsequent years, but did not catch another bass inside the marsh until 1936.

In September 1924, however, we began seriously to fish

the beach. On the first trip with the new outfit, Edward started two fish, both of which got off; but he saw them flash silver through the curl of the wave. Then he hooked one. I braved the surf with a homemade gaff, a gadget we soon found to be unnecessary, and hauled in a huge "barn-door" skate. Nothing daunted, we tried again and Edward finally landed a fine eight-pound bass. When the fish was beached, we all cheered lustily, the first of our well-known "bass yells" which can be heard as far as Provincetown. We did not realize at the time that this fish marked the beginning, or perhaps the recrudescence, of a sport which today brings many thousands of people to Cape Cod shores.

About two weeks later, having been occupied with shore bird and duck shooting in the interval, we struck it rich. There was a moderately heavy surf; the tide was ebbing through the Inlet, and the channel made close by the south point and out to the southeast. The incoming surf and outgoing ebb made an eddy at the peak of the beach, a spot that later came to be known for obvious reasons as the "Aquarium." On this occasion, taking turn and turn about with our one rod, we caught eight bass, weighing, in the aggregate, fifty-five pounds. Incidentally, in all the following years we never surpassed this record. Nor did we ever surpass the bass-eating record: fifty-five pounds of bass in one week!

The greatest fascination in surf fishing involved the problem of being in the right place at the right time. The ever-changing beach would never be the same two days running, and, in a week's time, could easily present an entirely different fishing proposition. During most of the years we fished the beach, there was, however, a general pattern. Starting

at the "Aquarium" and going south, one came to a high bar
which made well out to the southeast, with the Inlet channel running just to the north. At the height of tide, with a
moderate surf, fish could be caught right on top of this bar.
To the south there was usually a wide, rather deep eddy, and
fish often lay at the north end of it, just where the ebb swept
over the bar. This came to be known as "Fish Hog Point,"
again for obvious reasons. Still further south, there was another shoal; and here, not infrequently, rocks would appear.
Some years, there were so many rocks that fishing with our
rig became impossible; other years, almost all the rocks were
buried in the sand. Still further south came the houses, and
the Hot Dog Stand, and the main public swimming beach at
East Orleans. Although fish might be caught here on occasion, we rarely penetrated that far, largely in order to
avoid the picnicking crowds.

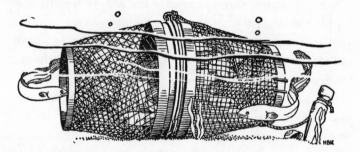

For bait we used small whole eels, and the first requisite
was to catch one. We spent hours trying to spear them with
eel and frog spears, but eventually found that clam-baited
minnow traps, set in one of the West Shore creeks, usually
produced eels of the required size. The next problem was to
string them. A single hook, with three or four links of "jack"

chain attached, could be threaded through the eel, so that the top link of chain lay just below the eel's nose. A close tie was made over the nose, and a homemade conical sinker, with a hole through the center, was passed over the line, to lie at the tie. If the tie was strongly made, the eel would be prevented from slipping down over the chain and hook. For it's an old adage that "a whirling eel gathers no bass." This was a dirty job; but after a little practice, we became quite proficient.

(Incidental note: If bluefish are around, they will bite off the tail and not get hooked, unless the hook is put within two or three inches of the tail tip.)

With the whole-eel rig, we could, with a fair breeze, cast out almost seventy-five yards. I never could manage an on-shore (easterly) wind if it had any heft. Even the jig fishermen always seemed to have much trouble with an easterly. The expert can determine exactly the proper weight of jig for his rod, and may then use it constantly. We, too, would get the feel of an optimum weight, and would try to fit our sinkers to the size of our eels; but, at best, we had to make an uncertain guess.

It is human nature to think that the best things are where you are not. The trout fisherman is always wishing he were on the other bank; and the surf caster thinks he must cast miles offshore. It is true that he thus may cover more water, but only exceptionally does it help him; for he has sacrificed a good natural bait for distance, and bass, if inclined to feed, are very likely to come right up onto the shelf. On the whole, we did better than most of our competitors, almost all of whom used some form of metal bait.

There was one nice-looking young man whom we frequently encountered on the beach. He had a beautiful overhand cast, and it was a delight to see his jig sail off into space, almost out of sight. We came to call him "The Blond Slugger." He used to catch a lot of bass, and may well have taken more fish off that beach than anyone else. However, we chose to attribute this rather more to his observance of Rule 1, and its corollary, Rule 2, than to his casting ability. (Rule 1: Be there when the fish are biting. Rule 2: He catches the most fish who does the most fishing.)

Some years ago, my children were attending the Unitarian Church in Chestnut Hill. They came home in breathless excitement. The new minister was The Blond Slugger! The Reverend Mr. Gesner, for he it was, has a deserved reputation as a bass fisherman.

By and large, we found the early ebb the most fruitful time to fish; and we probably caught most fish when the tide began to ebb strongly through the Inlet, some two hours after it had turned on the beach. Many fishermen forget that bass are night feeders. I have referred elsewhere to Rule 357: Bass tend to feed when the tide starts to ebb strongly. The corollary to this is Rule 358: If you wish to catch bass by daylight, fish when high water comes at morning and evening. I do not remember any of us taking a bass off the beach in the morning, that is, after full sunrise. Possible exceptions might occur during the late fall run.

Without a light, one necessarily must quit around "splash dark," when one can no longer see his bait hit the water. This is, however, the most likely time to land a fish. We started by carrying ordinary flashlights to help in freeing backlashes, and ended up by using a headlight with a belt-attached battery. With the latter, one can fish the darkest night. If a fish is hooked, the light is directed to the rod tip and the course of his run determined. When the fish is brought near the shelf, he can be spotted in the light and lifted home on an appropriate wave.

Backlashes are inevitable, though by paying close attention to the vagaries of the breeze they can largely be avoided. I have fished for four hours without a backlash; but this is a record to be spoken of in a hushed voice. Ordinarily, when fatigue begins, backlashes become more frequent. Usually they can be freed, but I had one which I stubbornly spent a week in undoing. Of course, I could have dismantled the reel and easily undone the thing, but having quit fishing, I was interested to see if it could be undone without removing the spool. A safety pin, always attached to one's shirt or elsewhere, is indispensable for undoing backlashes. When competition became heavy, I used to feel diffident about my prominently displayed safety pin, thinking that the connoisseur would say to himself, "Well, here's a dub"; nevertheless, I did not give up my pin, for, after all, the proof of the fishing is in the eating of bass for dinner.

As the years went by, we did more and more night fishing, in spite of the fact that to land a bass by daylight is far more satisfying than to do so at night. On an ordinary cloudless night, without a moon, you can see a good deal, once your eyes have become accommodated, but it should be remembered that frequent match flaring or flashlighting will greatly disturb such accommodation, and that it may take fifteen minutes or so to restore it. When you come to the rising, wade cautiously, bare-legged, into the wash, carefully wet your line by ever-lengthening casts, until a full cast can be made without a thumb burn. You can get the feel of the sea as it heaves back and forth, and you can see your bait against the sky to determine whether or not it is fouled. But you cannot very well tell about the runs and the eddies. Consequently, we frequently made a daylight survey of the area, and decided where and when to fish various places.

It is exciting to hook a fish at night. Quickly, two thumbs put pressure on the spool—not too much, for we believe in giving a fish his "head" and letting him run. But soon it becomes apparent that we do not know the direction of the run. One hand gropes for the battery switch, the other holds the rod and thumbs the reel at the same time. The headlight goes on, the line is seen to be dragging to the south. Patiently we wait, exert more thumb pressure, and finally the fish stops. For a brief moment nothing happens, and then suddenly the line goes limp. Lost? Then reel, reel for dear life; the fish is making a dead run inshore. If we are fortunate, and helped by the south drag of the line, we catch up to him before he shakes off. Then with taut line we carefully move to the south'ard until we are about opposite the fish. He is still strong, and makes short runs offshore. Our headlight now is turned toward the curling wave, and soon we see the umbrella-like dorsal fin and green back with silvery reflections as the fish turns and twists. But keep the pressure on, allow no slack! Work down toward the breaking wave, still with a taut line. Suddenly, a weakening of the strain tells us that the next wave will bring him in. It's a big wave. Back, back quickly, line taut, back up to the rising. Gradually the wave recedes, and there is our bass, twelve pounds of him, lying on the sand. If we are wise, we grab him with one thumb in his mouth, firmly holding the lower jaw. If we slip a finger under the gill covert, we may get a painful spine cut in so doing. Anyway, get him up out of reach of the sea, and never, never wash him until he is in the kitchen sink!

I do not advise fishing on a black night, a really black night. The blackest of all are nights of thick fog. You leave the car, after a precarious six-mile drive, on the bluff, and stumble down the quarter-mile sandy path to the beach, feeling your way gingerly with bare feet, noting sharp-pointed beach grass at the path edges. The roar of the surf grows louder, and suddenly you find yourself dropping off the shelf into the wash. This must be Fish Hog Eddy, you think. You keep well back, not being able to judge the thrust of the next wave, and reluctantly work to the north. You can see nothing, nothing at all except a vague whiteness near your feet. And incessantly the surf surges and retreats, now loudly roaring, now lisping; banging with gunshot suddenness one minute, the next filling the air with rushing sound. Finally, you stand at the peak of the bar, at high water. It looks all right, but then the first of three big waves breaks around your knees; the second, in spite of your backing up, wets your shorts; and the third thumps your belly. It's no good here, you say; and you work back to the south. Now the sea begins to talk. "Burr!" it says. And then, "Whitch!" And later, "Friends, ALL OUT, backlash, tea-party, rumble, bumble, lapse, wish, JUMP! STUMP! Broil steaks; boil and broil; LOOK OUT!"

About this time, your casting becomes erratic and your head is half the time turned over your shoulder. Suddenly the surf calls your name sharply: "WYMAN!" Quickly you reel in, stumble back over the path, and feel your way home through the fog to the Farm House. Here, after drying off in front of a small fire, you wonder at your own lack of courage. But just the same, leave the beach alone on a really dark night, whether it be fog or rain.

On the other hand, you can fish the beach on a full moon with almost the same satisfaction as in daylight. With a bright full moon, you can see your bait hit the water, and if fortunate enough to hook a fish, you can often play him without using your light.

I remember most vividly one clear night at full moon. We arrived at sunset, with the tide at two hours' flood. We made headquarters on a small beach-grass rise opposite Fish Hog Eddy, where we deposited our basket containing extra clothing, extra reels and equipment, and a snack to eat. It was a beautiful evening, with an orange moon rising out of a sea turbulent in spite of a fresh southwest breeze, and with the great beach stretching north and south to infinity. Well to the north, Nauset Light blinked somewhat ineffectually into the moon's brightness. We fished here and there without excitement, rested a bit, and ate a bit in front of a beach fire.

At high water, about eleven o'clock, I worked south to the bar below Fish Hog Eddy. I had previously noted a run inside this bar and figured the heavy surf rolling over it would run off to the north. I had made only two or three casts, when, just as my eel came over the bar into the run, a heavy fish grabbed it. He ran straight offshore. After he had taken off about a hundred yards of line I began to worry and put the pressure on. Finally he stopped, and then came back, straight in. It seemed like hours of frantic reeling before I caught up with him at the shelf; and my feeling of relief that he was still hooked was almost shattering. He made several more runs, but I became more rugged and made it difficult for him. He hung off the curl of the breakers for a long while, but at last the strain was too much for him, and he came up docilely on the wash of a wave. He looked magnificent as he lay on the beach, and I felt sorry for him. However, I lugged him to headquarters, and came back to try again.

On my first cast, I hooked another which felt and acted exactly like a twin fish. He ran out one hundred yards or more of line; I stopped him. And then I began to wonder what we'd do with fifty-odd pounds of fish in the fish box. At this point, like his predecessor, he ran straight inshore. I never caught up with him. He must have dropped the hook at the shelf, for I did not feel any drag until then, when I ruefully reeled in a bedraggled eel, and resolved never again to worry about the fish box.

My fish weighed twenty-four pounds, my biggest. When I cleaned him, I found twelve spike mackerel in his stomach, which must have increased his weight by at least one pound. Except for brother Harry's twenty-eight-and-a-half-pounder, this is the biggest fish we have caught. Some day, we hope to hook into a monster, say seventy-five pounds or more, remembering that one of one hundred eight pounds or better was caught on a hand line off this beach many years ago. But such fancies remain for the future.

My most satisfying experience occurred late one September afternoon. My daughter, Char, and I arrived at the beach with the tide at a little less than half-flood. Already the sun at our backs was so low that the dune shadows reached the wet sand. As we reconnoitered from the rising, there was no sign of fish. I noted a large rock, prominent for the first time in several years, less than a full cast offshore, its peak showing through the crest of a moderate surf. The current sweeping to the north was making an observable eddy to the north of the rock.

"If I were a bass," I said to Char, "I would lie in the eddy behind that rock."

The next question was how to get my eel through the eddy without fouling the rock. I decided to cast directly over the rock and then to run north down the beach. Fortunately I made a good cast well beyond and directly over the rock; then, without touching either clutch or click, I clamped a thumb on the reel spool, and ran down the beach as fast as I could. I had taken perhaps fifteen steps, when I was fetched up short by the solid pull of my line. Then zing! Out it went. I finally managed to set the click, and felt better; but it was some time before I stopped this fish's run. I kept trying to work him to the north out of the rocks, and eventually was lucky enough to land him. He turned out to be a fine fourteen-pounder, a fighter beyond his weight.

Our best year was 1932. We did not have to fish at night, and caught most of our fish in the late afternoon, at sunset, or at dawn. During this season, we took bass over a very shoal bar in the white wash of outer breaking surf, at near low water. I remember introducing a friend one day to the fascination and annoyances of surf casting. He tried a cast, and had an immediate backlash which pulled his eel back into the wash at his feet. He had just freed his reel when his line started out at express rate, and shortly after, he landed a twelve-pound bass.

During our few weeks at the Farm House in 1932, we

caught twenty-eight bass, weighing in the aggregate two hundred and ninety-two pounds. These fish were mostly caught on whole eels, or, in some cases, on eelskins. (The skin of an eel, necessarily turned inside out by the process of skinning, is bright blue. When strung over a hook *and chain*, much as in stringing a whole eel, it makes a killing bait both for bass and bluefish, so tough that it takes even several bluefish to cut it up sufficiently to require restringing.) We got

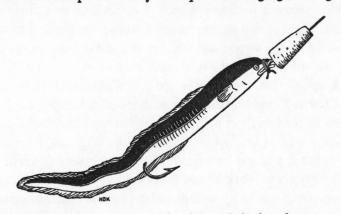

the feeling in 1932 that catching bass off the beach was easy once you developed the know-how. We spent many of the following years getting over this feeling.

As the years rolled by, we did more and more night fishing. In the daytime, as brother Harry put it, the beach came to look like an alder swamp, so numerous were the rods. It was not only impossible to fish the right place at the right time; it was even difficult to find any room at all to put in. So, more and more, we fished at night or in the very early morning hours. Eventually, we gave it up altogether. Now, only seldom do I fish the beach, and then usually on the north side of the Inlet.

One September evening in 1936, my wife and I were sitting on the Farm House platform. The sun had disappeared, leaving lovely soft sunset colors behind it. To the east a huge orange moon, squashed at top and bottom and bulging on the flanks, had just cleared the dunes. There was a light westerly air. Suddenly I smelt that strong, cucumber-like smell of feeding fish. Quickly, we walked the hundred yards to a spot that overlooked the Salt Pond. We saw what seemed like large fish smashing the quiet water.

The next afternoon, having tied some white feathers to a trout hook, I began casting with my four-ounce fly rod. Before long, a fish roared out and started off with my line. Unfortunately it was old rotten line and it soon parted. The next morning I was out at dark, and, after waiting in the boathouse for a thunderstorm to pass by, I again began fly-casting, this time with about forty yards of nine-thread Cuttyhunk salt-water line. It made casting quite difficult, but I was sure it would hold. There was a light northeast breeze, and occasional light rain. I started at the windward shore and let the boat drift off. I soon had a rise and was fast to a fighting fish. My excitement was intense as I finally brought him close to the net, for I still did not know what kind of fish he was. Great was my delight when he turned out to be a nice bass, about two and one-half pounds. After this, I hooked a fish on almost every drift, and came home with four, weighing from one and one-half to three and one-half pounds. It was the most magnificent fishing I had ever had.

Since then we have done more and more fishing "inside," until now we rarely fish the beach. We have not had another visitation of a two-year brood that has anywhere nearly

equalled that of 1936. This was the time that bass appeared
in places where they had not been seen for years, such as
Duxbury Bay and Newburyport Harbor. We have caught
many two-year-olds (one and one-half to two pounds) in
following years, but have had no such tremendous runs.

Our outfit has improved. I have a reel that carries about
twenty yards of waxed line and one hundred yards of fine
silk backing. The casting line has to be washed immediately
after being used in salt water, or it will rot overnight. We
fish usually with bucktail streamers with a large hook. For
the most part we troll, always out of a canoe. One could
fish for bass much as one does for Atlantic salmon, with a
couple of guides to hold the canoe over the riffles while one
casts ahead of the boat. We cover so much more water by
trolling, and find so much else of interest by stirring around,
that we rarely stop to fly-cast.

We find fish on shallow sand riffles, and on runs over bars.
One gets practiced in seeing fish under water, smelling them,
and noting their presence by the action of terns or by the
way herring gulls are sitting around. In the canoe we run up
close to many fish. We may see, on a calm day, a tiny ripple
presumably caused by a minnow. We come to within six
feet of it when, with a roar, ten or twelve bass boil away.
The minnow was the second dorsal spine of a bass, just showing above the surface of the water. Such bass never bite;
hence the adage: "A boiling bass never bites." Sometimes the
fish will not show at all but will unexpectedly strike. At
other times a feeding school will appear, and, if we reach
them in time, a strike is certain. A feeding bass makes a sucking sound, which in the distance has the quality of a pistol
shot. Not infrequently a school of bass will harry bait with-

out actually feeding. On such occasions they will often roll almost clear of the water or flip their tails way out. We call this "golloping"—"A golloping bass never bites"—and very disappointing it is, too.

Quiet is essential. Even rowing makes too much noise, and outboard motors will effectively stop all feeding. I have seen this on several occasions. Twice I have seen the whole area between the Beach Channel and Broad Creek alive with feeding bass. Each time, when a passing outboard came by, every fish stopped feeding. One time, the fish started feeding again after an interval of twenty minutes; the other, they quit for the day. Some bass can be taken from outboards when the fish are in deep water, but I am convinced motor boats will ruin shallow water fishing.

Bass are an unpredictable fish. Just as you think you have their ways figured out, they will do something entirely different. We have to keep changing our rules, and indeed can only be sure of Rules 1 and 2. Of one thing I am fairly certain: bass get sick of feeding on the same kind of bait. I have seen them suddenly stop feeding on pogies (menhaden), for instance, even though the marsh was full of them. At such times, they start feeding on shrimps, crabs, and worms; and then they are very hard to catch on any lure designed to resemble bait. Like the human infant if left to its own devices, the bass seems to feel an instinctive urge for some previously missing food element, and suddenly changes its habits. Even the shape and taste of bass may change considerably in the course of a few weeks.

We have never successfully developed a method of shrimp fishing, though I am sure it is possible. So far, we have tried only half-heartedly, and soon have tired of being restricted to one spot. The killing spinner-and-worm bait can only be used in deep water, and I have not used it since the old days when the children were small. By and large, we get enough fish to eat, and this is all we want. They range in size from one and one-half pounds at sixteen inches, to our "inside" record of eleven and one-half pounds, caught on our four-ounce fly rod. My wife caught one of nine and one-half pounds on this same rod, at night. It was a tribute to her ability that this fish was landed from the bottom of a canoe without springing the rod, for when a bass is brought close to the canoe, likely as not he will dive under it. Then the rod butt must quickly go overhead, and it's no joke holding a nine and one-half pound fish with your arms extended straight over your head.

My wife has developed a new technique to prevent reel overruns. This consists in allowing the reel handle to thump lightly the palm of the hand. Strange as it may seem, absolute control can be gained in this way under conditions where direct thumbing is impossible.

Most of our bass are females. Since I have been sexing them, all over ten pounds and over ninety per cent of the smaller fish have been females. I do not know where the males keep themselves, but I suspect they remain in warmer waters. I have never seen a gravid bass; they are said to spawn in May or June, months when I have done little fishing. Certainly we have never seen bass fry in this latitude, so that if bass do spawn in these waters, it is unlikely that the eggs hatch.

Being a coastal fish, bass are easily netted out. It seems to me the greatest good to the greatest number requires strict control of netting. This must be on a federal basis; or at least netting must be controlled in those waters where bass breed—especially in the Chesapeake Bay area—if we are to have a plentiful supply.

I have written at some length of my friend, *Roccus lineatus*, because I consider him the king of all fishes. Judging from the number of people who pursue him, many others must agree with this opinion. However, when any of the Farm House crew are approaching the boathouse at the mouth of the Salt Pond Creek, in the dark of night, with no fish in the stern of the canoe to drag it down a little, they can be heard muttering. Could one be close enough, he might make out some mumbled, oft-repeated words: "Those Consecrated Dunderheads!"

---

7. *Morning Interlude*

ONE DAY in late September, I hauled myself out of bed shortly after four o'clock, Farm House time (the clocks had been officially retarded the day before). A full orange moon was slowly slipping behind the western horizon, and there was a faint pink color to the eastern sky as I left the house. Orion hung to the southeast surrounded by its galaxy of brilliant stars. Twinkling Sirius, not far above the southeastern horizon, was the brightest star in the sky, brighter than any planet.

It was cold down by the creek, especially so for bare feet, as I put the canoe into the water. The water itself was relatively warm, but that made matters worse when I hauled my feet into the canoe. As I worked down the channel, I could hear ducks quacking. A fast-flying teal skipped across the bow, silhouetted against the now reddening eastern sky. Not a breath of wind stirred the surface of the water. I surprised a night heron close to the channel edge, and he flew clumsily away, no doubt as fast as he could, protesting loudly with a series of outlandish squawks that violated the morning's quiet.

It was light enough, by the time I rounded Porchy Bar, to see shore birds on the flats. So many were there, that the flats seemed to be in constant motion. There were large flocks of black-billed sanderling, white in their winter plumage, the wave-chasing "peep" of the beaches; many red-backed sandpipers, the English "dunlin," that hardy, curved-billed peep of the winter marshes; and, strangely enough, knots, whose spring-plumaged chestnut-colored breasts have given them the common name of "redbreast." There was also a good sprinkling of the so-called black-bellied plover, whose bellies are always white, though their breasts may be black. Most of these were pale all over, perhaps the young of the year. They ran rather sedately over the upper bars, searching for large sea worms, stopping suddenly, now and then, to look about. And in those shallow, muddy places, bands of greater yellowlegs formed ranks and chased schools of minnows into shallow water where they could be caught and eaten.

I saw a lot of black ducks for this time of year, one hundred and eight to be exact. As I came by in the canoe, they would jump from the water with a roar that shattered the still air. Back on the marsh, I could hear an occasional quack, and sometimes that low "chuck-a-duck-a-duck" call that contented ducks make.

Just as I came to Broad Creek, the shore birds all took to the air, some of them making a queerly shrill call that could only mean a dangerous hawk was about. I soon found the culprit. A sharp-shinned hawk had struck a small peep down into the water. The peep was alive, probably wing-broken, and the hawk was trying to secure his prey. However, three large herring gulls, uttering coarse cries, attacked the hawk, and after several futile passes he disappeared. The gulls *may* have been motivated by a desire to save a feathered friend. I wish I could believe so. But I am terribly afraid they wanted to devour the peep themselves. Unfortunately, I did not determine the point, for at this moment my reel suddenly began to sing. I lost the bass, but when this tragedy occurred, the tide had carried me far down the channel.

I startled several bass in the shoal water where the Beach House Run comes out to the Main Channel. They scooted off, humping the water up like submarines about to surface. On my way back up, I saw a bass feeding on a school of pogies in the deep water close to the edge of Porchy Marsh. A quawk, happily perched on a broken-off piece of sedge, stood motionless, his beak a quarter inch from the water, waiting for the bass to drive the pogies within striking distance. As I edged up in the canoe, his dilemma was ludicrous. Should he wait one more moment for the expected morsel, or should prudence take precedence over appetite? Prudence prevailed and he took off with a protesting croak. Neither he nor I got any fish.

It was a very low water—"low dreen" as the saying goes; but I elected to go back up the Minister's Channel, knowing well that the mouth of it would be dry. I was glad I did. As I silently poled the canoe up by Minister's Point, I came upon a green-winged teal. He seemed quite tame, and appeared to be lonely, for he kept uttering a queer little laryngeal quack and did not fly until I came within thirty yards of him. Before he flew, he drifted onto the flat, apparently in order to

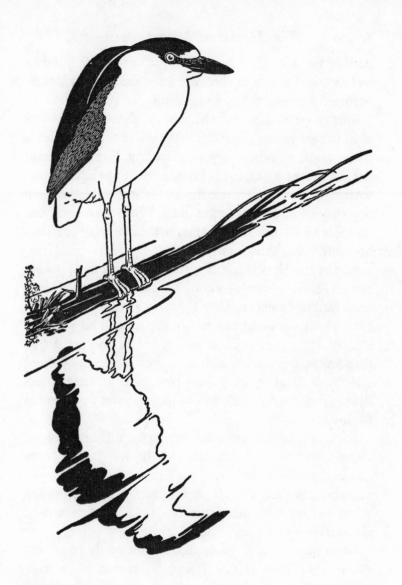

HENRY
BUGBEE
KANE

get a better take-off. When he did go, he took off as only a teal can, and not until then did I see the beautiful, buff-bordered green speculum on his wing.

Further on up, just at the head of the channel, I poked up close to two young pintails. They were very loath to leave the soft ooze in which they were feeding. First they swam out into deeper water, but as I approached I was interested to see that they worked back to the flat—just as did the teal—so that they could make a better jump. When they went, one jumped to the north and the other to the south, which shows how little wind there was.

Just as the pintails left, I was startled to hear a golden plover. I tried to imitate his note, but only frightened a black duck feeding behind a grassy point not twenty yards away. He jumped a good fifteen feet in the air, and his very red legs, shining in the sun, his large size, and his sleek and glossy dark feathering marked him as one of the large "redleg" variety. Meanwhile the golden plover, darker and faster-flying cousin to the black-bellied plover, lit on a nearby flat for my benefit.

Fortunately for me, the obstructing flat at the head of the channel was wet and soft, and I easily dragged the canoe across, the only hazard being the danger of stepping on an upended razor-clam shell. One gets used to "feeling the way" when walking with bare feet in the mud, and I negotiated the portage without accident.

From there back to the boathouse, I leisurely poked the canoe in shallow water, watching the bottom in the now bright sunlight. In the inside channel between the Cedar Bank Channel and First Hummock, I saw a "windowpane" flounder, or sand dab, lying still, heading upstream, his only motion being the opening and shutting of his large mouth as he gulped down the minnows that I drove past him. As broad as he is long, you can, if you hold him up, see the light shine through him. How could such a greedy fish remain so thin?

Still further up, I came upon Horseshoe-crab-ville, where the bottom seemed literally to be paved with them. And finally, I poked up into the Salt Pond Creek, where I saw some huge oysters that are excellent when baked.

And so up the hill to the Farm House—a curious, recurring ache in the pit of the stomach suggesting that more food is in order. It is nine-thirty, Farm House time. Clock time means little here at the Farm House. Dinner will be at a quarter to eleven. Then a snooze, and after that perhaps a go at some of the things on the "thing" list. Supper will be at half past four or so, and later, possibly a sunset and night expedition. Would the cold meat of freshly caught blue crabs, with just a dab of mayonnaise, taste good tomorrow?

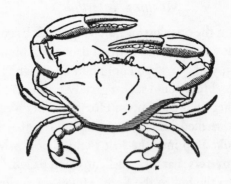

8. Blue Crabbing

ONE of our more exciting Farm House expeditions is a blue crab hunt.

Blue crabs are our largest crab. The shells measure six to seven inches across their longest diameter. Horseshoe crabs don't count, and the body of those large deep water spider crabs is considerably smaller than that of a blue crab, even though their diameter from leg to leg is greater. Blue crabs have paddles on their hindermost pair of legs and can scull either to right or to left with amazing speed. They keep their forward great claw bent at the elbow and let the aft one drag out straight astern. When they reverse their direction, which they can do with extraordinary rapidity, the previously dragging claw is bent and the other allowed to drag.

These crabs are vicious!

I wish I could think of a stronger word for it, and perhaps some day I will be able to. They are armed with two heavy claws, each of which terminates in needle-pointed, strong jaws which are studded with tooth-like excrescences. When a blue crab makes a pass at something, he brings his claws together in a flashing arc. If he misses, the claws meet with a loud crack.

Furthermore, he appears to have double-jointed shoulder joints. In the case of most crabs, one can watch for the chance to grab him firmly by the hind end, thumb on top and fingers beneath; the crab then futilely gnashes his teeth well forward of one's tender digits. Not so the blue crab. He can bring his claws well up over his back. I seem to remember as a boy carrying blue crabs in my fingers, but I can't do it any more. In my old age, the near miss of those clashing jaws is too much for me and I invariably drop the crab—which always leads to further difficulties.

We have not always had blue crabs here. They are warm water crustaceans, and are not regular inhabitants of the Gulf of Maine. Doctor Bigelow (*Fishes of the Gulf of Maine*, Bigelow and Welsh) in his definition of the Gulf of Maine includes that part of Cape Cod lying north of Monomoy Point. We at Eastham fall within this limit. At any rate, while blue crabs have always been common along the south shore of the Cape from Stage Harbor to Woods Hole, their appearance here in the Nauset Marsh is of very recent date. It is only within the last ten—or perhaps more nearly five— years that they have been abundant.

Probably there have been previous periods of abundance here; and I doubt if this fluctuation is due to any such condition as water salinity or water temperature. As in all fish, periods of general abundance and scarcity are reflected, at the limits of their range, by their presence or absence. This is particularly noticeable in the case of bluefish, which, during periods of abundance, appear off the east shore of the outer Cape and even north and west of it. But during periods of relative scarcity they disappear from the outer Cape and often from Buzzards Bay as well.

I am not sure just when blue crabs appear in spring, probably in May. However, we have never fished for them before July. This is by far the most exciting time, for the warm water puts these huge monsters on their mettle. They are then not only extremely agile, but the warmth seems to annoy them and they will snap at the least provocation.

In October, on the other hand, the cold water makes them sluggish and consequently much easier to catch. Furthermore, after a night in the icebox, they can even be handled with impunity. But caution! Do not leave them long in a warm kitchen, or you may rue your overconfidence.

One way of getting blue crabs is to spear them. However, we consider this an inferior method. Not only is it definitely timorous; it also kills the crab. As my boyhood friend and mentor, our boatman, Mel Marble, often pointed out, one should not eat crabs or lobsters unless one has seen that they were alive before they were cooked. I confess that I do not always follow this rule, but it is a good one nevertheless.

Our method is to net them with a long-handled, shallow, wide-meshed net. And we net them at night. It is true that they can be found in the daytime, but at night there will be ten in shoal water where otherwise there would be but one. The required conditions are a flat, or near flat, calm, and low water in the Salt Pond at a reasonable hour of the night. This means that low water must occur about an hour and a half or so after sunset.

For night crabbing we use the three-battery headlights,

much like a miner's light, that we use for night bassing. We prefer to go out in a fairly heavy boat designed as a ducking float. A two-man expedition may take the canoe. This greatly increases the sporting element in the proposition, but is not recommended for beginners. A crew of four is the limit; and since we have only one net it has to be constantly passed back and forth.

The crabbing boat always has some water in it and the bottom consequently has a smooth, slightly slimy consistency. It is one of the rules of the game to go barefoot. The big fish basket is the crab receptacle, and is placed amidships.

The basket is important. Once we forgot it and had to use the bucket which always resides in the boathouse. All went well for a time. But our quota was sixteen crabs, and towards the end of the trip it became a great problem to keep the crabs within the bucket. This was solved by immediately placing the seat (of the boat, not of the pants) over the bucket as soon as a crab was released from the net. Even this was not one hundred per cent effective. Every now and again would come the cry, "Loose Crab!" whereupon all hands would take to forward or after decking, a feat requiring no little sense of balance.

The time is nine-thirty of a mid-July evening. The tide has still an hour to ebb from the Salt Pond Creek and there is only the slightest afterglow in the western sky. It is flat calm. There are four of us and we soon have the "double" afloat in the creek. This time we have remembered to bring along the basket. The Old Man in the stern takes an oar and begins slowly poking the boat up the creek. He tries to keep the boat in less than a foot of water so that everything on the bottom can be clearly seen.

Suddenly the bow man shudders. A huge eel, about ready for its long Bermuda trip, has appeared in the sharp focus of the headlight. As we pass by, the eel lies quietly, apparently unafraid of the light. Green crabs, spider crabs, hermit crabs all are seen; but no blue crabs. Our quota is sixteen and somebody states that this year there are no blue crabs.

Then comes the cry: "Crab ho!"

The oarsman tries to hold the boat steady. There is some debate as to whether the crab is big enough. It is; the net is passed to the one amidships who is nearest. Very carefully the net is lowered to a strategic position just aft of the crab, and a quick thrust is made. But the crab is quicker. All the lights are now focussed on him, and as the crab sculls his way over the edge of the net and flies off into the darkness of the pond a concerted groan goes up. Then someone says, "He was too small anyway."

The oarsman gives the boat a shove upstream, without comment.

"Crab ho!"

There's a huge one, caught in the shallow water of the bar. It's the bowman's chance. This time his quick thrust is successful; the crab is entangled in the mesh of the net and is swung inboard over the basket. The net is overturned, but the crab persists in hanging onto the twine with a vise-like grip. Finally the Old Man bats him off into the basket with his oar. There the crab scrabbles around threateningly, but curiously does not seem to be able to climb over the side.

Now we have to paddle through deep water around the peak of the bar which drops steeply down for fifteen or twenty feet. Soon, however, we come to shoal water again off the Nauset Spring. (Nauset Spring water is "good for what ails ye; an' if there ain't nothin' ails ye, it's a good perventative.") And again comes the cry of "Crab ho!" This crab, too, is caught, but unfortunately, as he drops into the basket, one of his great claws is left hanging over the edge. Before this matter can be remedied, over the side he goes, and that petrifying cry goes up: "Loose Crab!"

It usually takes a male to meet such a situation and this time the Old Man is the only one. He sits down on the afterdeck with his feet draped over the gunn'ls. He waits until the crab, on one of his peregrinations, comes aft. Then the Old Man suddenly pins the crab down to the bottom of the boat by firmly pressing his thumb on the crab's back. So pinioned, the crab cannot reach up and over. Cautiously, the Old Man sneaks his fingers under the crab and, with a quick motion, tosses him into the basket. Should the basket be missed, the Old Man is in for a certain amount of caustic comment.

It is off Bass Cove and Sea Lettuce Point just beyond that we do our greatest business. Things get going fast and furiously, and by the time we get to the public bathing beach we are only two short of our quota. When at last we return to the boathouse, our batteries are becoming weak and our energy is fast disappearing. But we think we have our quota of sixteen, although our counts under such conditions are notoriously inaccurate.

Among the sixteen, we know there will be several softshelled crabs. Some of these will be so soft that they might be cooked whole in deep fat. However, the problem of how to retrieve them from that seething basket has never been solved. We put the whole basket in the fish box, knowing well that those poor soft-shells will, before morning, be badly mangled.

Next day, as soon as the breakfast things have been washed and put away, two large kettles are a little more than half filled with water and put on the fire to boil. It always amazes me how long this takes. No matter how early we get up, it is usually well after eleven before the kettle comes to a full boil. The basket is then removed from the fish box, and with the aid of the fire tongs, about eight crabs are transferred to each of the boiling kettles and the covers are clamped over them as quickly as possible.

It is important not to overestimate the capacity of the kettle. I remember, when I was a boy, seeing my mother supervise the boiling of a mess of blue crabs my friend and I had caught. There was a huge kettle of boiling water on the stove, and the cook and her helpers, of which in those days there were several, were standing around watching. Mother directed my friend and me to dump the crabs into the kettle. We had them in a crab car and proceeded to do as we were bidden. Unfortunately, Mother did not realize how many crabs there were in the car. The next moment there was chaos. Crabs crawling nimbly over the hot stove and falling to the floor. Crabs under the tables. Crabs under the chairs. Crabs in every corner. The women shrieked and quickly repaired to the top of the kitchen table, where they stood with their skirts lifted. It took at least an hour for my friend and me to restore order. However, I have never forgotten the crab Newburg we had that night.

I have no qualms when it comes to the ethics of putting

live crustaceans into boiling water. I understand that recently the Massachusetts Society for the Prevention of Cruelty to Animals has recommended dunking lobsters or crabs in a concentrated salt solution which is said to cause their painless demise. I have seen nothing in the literature suggesting that a crab or lobster suffers less when dunked in a strong salt solution than when dunked in boiling water. In fact, the latter is undoubtedly the quickest form of death there is.

Our crabs have been put into the kettles of boiling water and the fire made as hot as possible. They are boiled eleven minutes, counting from the time when the water again starts to boil, then ladled out into the big colander and put into the sink where cool water is pumped over them. The legs are torn off and thrown away, and the big claws saved. The outer shells are removed by lifting the V-shaped shield on the under side and prying off the top shells with the thumbs. Let no man, no matter how powerful, try to break the shell in two by brute strength. The resulting splash will not only cover himself and all the guests, but the ceiling and walls as well.

When the shell has been removed, the gills are peeled off and the inside matter poked out and washed away. The crab is now ready for picking.

This is best done by first breaking the body in two, pressing inward, and then breaking each half into smaller pieces. With a thin-bladed knife the flesh is teased out of its cells. Finally the claws are cracked with the pliers and the big hunks of meat removed with the knife. Great care must be taken not to include any chitinous material with the meat.

One piece of shell may spoil what otherwise would be the dish supreme.

The picking process usually takes an hour and a quarter to an hour and a half, no matter how numerous the crabs. For we figure three to four crabs to the person; consequently, the more crabs, the more people to do the picking. My Baltimore friend scoffs at this small individual quota and states that some of his neighbors will eat ten to twelve crabs at a sitting. I do not wish to doubt my friend's veracity, but I do doubt the thoroughness with which these crabs are eaten.

In any event, four crabs apiece, prepared by our method, is usually more than we can eat. We put the meat in the refrigerator and wait as long as our patience will allow. Then we sit down with a pile of clear crab meat before us, some mayonnaise mixed with milk or cream on the side, and set to.

And so ends the crabbing expedition—in silence, except for various and sundry chomping noises.

Yes, it's a fine sport and well worth the trouble. If you get the chance, just try it sometime.

9. *Do-Nothing Day*

JUST how one tells when a "do-nothing" day arrives, I have never been able to make out. There is some combination involving both weather elements and human physiology which, when it occurs, makes it clear to all that such a day is at hand. Although it may come at any time of year, it may, of course, be masked by some urgent necessity such as duck shooting or bass fishing. Even then, an extremely severe do-nothing day may show up, causing everyone, often somewhat to his surprise, to give up plans for the usual strenuous activities.

It is September. A before-breakfast weather observation has revealed a sparklingly clear day. A deep blue sky already is beginning to be spotted with fluffy white cumulus clouds, carried before a fresh northwest breeze. Just the day for energy and activity, you say? No! It soon becomes apparent that this is a do-nothing day.

Breakfast is prepared in a leisurely fashion, starting with a large glass of freshly prepared orange juice, squeezed in the old-fashioned blue china contraption with a hump in the middle, not in the modern metal gadget. This is followed by fried eggs, bacon, and toast, and topped off with a large cup of coffee—made as coffee should be made, in a regulation coffeepot. We sit around the table for a long time, sipping coffee and enjoying a smoke while talk drifts to this subject and that. Through the south windows we look out across the hill where waves of yellow-brown grass, borne by a fresh breeze, seem to climb up and over. After a long time, first one person and then another stirs, and eventually the dishes get washed.

"What'll we do today?" someone asks.

There is a long silence.

"Nothing," comes the reply, most likely from me.

And nothing it is.

Then comes a period of sitting on the edge of the low platform on the south side of the house, with bird glasses near at hand. A gray marsh hawk, looking almost blue in the bright light, follows his customary beat between the hills and down across the little meadow by the Salt Pond Creek. He sails along close to the grass with very little effort, and sometimes hangs almost motionless on an updraft as he scans the grass for sign of mouse or other succulent morsel. Suddenly, over toward the Cedar Bank, the crows begin a great racket. From all directions more crows can be seen, flying fast and true to the scene of the disturbance. Shortly, the cause of all this commotion becomes thoroughly annoyed. A very large red fox, pursued by fifty chattering crows, comes out of the cedars, lopes down through the hollow and up back of the barn, and disappears through Mrs. Doane's or-

chard. Undoubtedly, he will cross the road and make for the
thicket the other side of Robbins' Pond.

Now butterflies claim our attention. The stunning black
swallowtail comes floating gracefully by and obligingly
lights on the short grass not far away. She seems not a bit
skittish and will allow a quiet approach to within a few feet,
as she spreads her lovely iridescent wings to catch the
warmth of the sun and to show off the brilliant coral spot in
her lower wing. Her mate is never very far away. He is perhaps not so beautiful as his colorful spouse, but he carries a
fine yellow band near the margin of his wings that contrasts
sharply with his otherwise dark coloring. He is a great
fighter, too, as any black swallowtail who makes the mistake
of wandering too close will soon find out. We see occasionally the tiger swallowtail, and the powerful monarch is not
uncommon, but the black swallowtail belongs particularly
to the Farm House.

The American copper should perhaps be considered the
Farm House butterfly. He has coppery-red wings, speckled
with black, and is very tame, though he makes a fast getaway
when disturbed. He has been attracted in great abundance
by the presence of large areas of sorrel. The grayling, with
eye-like spots on his wings, annoys us by his habit of closing
his wings when resting, but he is, withal, a charming butterfly. Occasionally we see a painted beauty or his close relative,
the cosmopolite, a streak of beautiful pink contrasting
sharply with the dull gray of the under surface of his
wings.

It is fun to study the butterflies in the field and to try to
identify them without collecting them. In many instances
this can be done, especially with the help of bird glasses; in

others, only the family, such as the skippers, can be identified.

It is time, now, for the day's major activity. This consists of a long walk down the hill to the boathouse, a matter of two hundred and fifty yards or so. For a while we sit on the boathouse platform. The tide has started to flood up the Salt Pond Creek and the lower flats are rapidly being covered. Terns, finding the water of the bay too rough for successful fishing, circle around and around in the lee of the hill, and then make their way up the creek to see what is doing in the Salt Pond.

We spend a long time inspecting them closely in the attempt to identify the species. The arctic tern, with his bright red bill, has a somewhat more graceful flight, looks a trifle larger, and has some characteristic arrangement of the black edging to the outer wing feathers, all of which make him relatively easy to differentiate. The roseate tern, so named because of the beautiful pink wash on his spring-plumaged breast, can be told by his black bill and somewhat smaller size. He also seems a little whiter. The common tern's bill is usually tipped with black and he is not so regal a bird as his cousin, the Arctic, nor quite so graceful. The young of the year, with white forehead and rather stubby wings, are so much alike we do not try to tell them apart. A possible exception might be the Forster's tern, whose offspring have a black line through the eye, but one must be sure that it does not run all the way around the back of his head, as it does in some of the commoner species.

As the tide rises further, a steady stream of shore birds begins to pass by. They are of all sizes. Flocks of tiny least and semipalmated sandpipers turn and twist with incredible rapidity as they make their way to windward. Fast-flying black-bellied plover, often in more or less of a line, are interspersed with straggling flocks of big winter yellowlegs whose long yellow legs trail out beyond their tail tips.

In about half an hour the flight is over. We take to watching the antics of a very large orange and black wasp with a long, narrow waist—one of the sphecid wasps. We have previously noted a slanting, half-inch hole in front of which the sand is piled up in a little mound. This wasp has succeeded in killing (or drugging?) one of those big flying grasshoppers which are so common down here, and is obviously trying to drag the monster, which is twice her length and three times her weight, to the hole. The distance is six feet, and what to the wasp must seem like a jungle of grass and weeds separates her from the hole. Her method is to grasp the grasshopper near his head with her front legs, and back up towards her destination. Unfortunately, this largely deprives her of the use of her best eyes, her delicate antennae, and she frequently goes astray. Then she lets go her prey and makes a reconnaissance, after which she hurries back. In fact, the most striking thing about her is her panic of haste.

Nothing else can be done until we have seen the feat accomplished. After a long time, the hole is reached and the
wasp backs down, dragging the grasshopper after her. For a
while nothing happens. Then the wasp comes out minus the
grasshopper. How she managed to by-pass him in the tunnel remains a mystery. Feverishly, she starts plugging up the
hole, using the mound in front, until it is completely plugged.
Then she circles around a few times, comes back once
and again to tamp down the plug, and finally flies away—
where, we do not know. I suppose she has laid her eggs in
the tunnel, and, having supplied her future offspring with
food, has gone off with the feeling that she has accomplished
her mission.

There follow a few desultory remarks about the desira-
bility of cleaning up the boathouse, restringing and painting
the decoys, mending the gear, and so forth, but no one makes
any such move. There is also some talk of a swim, but the
air is too cool and comfortable, and the flood tide, with its
flotsam and jetsam, does not look inviting. Besides, the sun
is in the south, and the inner man begins to grumble a bit.
So we wander back up the hill.

When we reach the house, the surrounding cedars are
found to be alive with birds. They turn out to be pine
warblers—olive-brown little birds with conspicuous white
patches on their outer tail feathers. The driveway is filled
with chipping sparrows; there are three robins in the thick,
unpruned apple tree by the barn; and five bluebirds are sitting on the barn roof. This curious combination of species—
the thrushes (robins and bluebirds), the sparrows, and the
warblers—is a very common one here at this time of year,

and I have come to realize that it represents a very definite migratory unit.

For instance, you may find such a group of birds busily feeding among the pitch pines near the road north of the "Quawkery." Suddenly the robins and bluebirds fly up to the telephone wires, or to the top of a large cedar, and begin to call. The sweet warbling note of the bluebirds is especially reassuring. For several minutes they continue their calls, while little "chips" and other very faint calls grow in volume from all about. After three or four minutes, the robins and bluebirds take off in a leisurely way toward the southwest. The little call notes increase in intensity, as one after another the pine warblers follow their leaders. Soon the chipping sparrows join the flight, intermingling with the last of the warblers but definitely forming a rear guard. It takes about ten minutes for the whole flock to get under way. At the end of that time, the last sparrow has disappeared and the pine trees are deserted.

It is perfectly obvious that the bigger birds, the robins and the bluebirds, are leading the way and shepherding their flock toward warmer climes. I do not think they cover much distance at one time, at least during the day, but, day or night, they keep in touch with each other by constant calling. Some still night, during the height of the migration, sit outdoors and listen. You may suddenly become conscious of a constant chorus of chirps and calls coming out of the darkness from overhead. And should you hear the soft warble of a bluebird, you may imagine him encouraging his trusting group of smaller brethren and guiding them to their destination. The thought of this relationship has somehow given me great comfort. Through the dark passages that must sometimes be negotiated, what better guide could one have than the cheerful, sagacious robin or the unpretentious, caretaking, sensible bluebird?

The time has come to prepare the big meal, a process that will take one and one half to two hours. We have very definite ideas about food and how it should be prepared. We like it simple but properly cooked. We do not go in for rare spices, unusual combinations, difficult sauces and such things. We like good fresh fish of all kinds, or shellfish, or ducks. Bass head chowder is our specialty, but we can make a good, simple quahog or clam chowder that you will not soon forget. And by chowder, I mean chowder and not a kind of glorified tomato bouillon.

Today's dinner is to be broiled striped bass and creamed potatoes—nothing more. Some of us may feel the need of topping this off with one or two of those cookies that the Orleans bakery specializes in, and, of course, coffee, a fortified edition of the morning's brew, is essential.

The trick about broiling bass is to have the fire in the stove at just the right point. This requires a certain judgment when the wind is due west, for under such circumstances there is for some reason a draft which sweeps down over the peak of the roof and sends puffs of smoke swirling out around the edges of the stove covers.

Fortunately, on this day, the wind has a definite northerly slant and the stove will draw. The fire is started, and while it is getting under way, the fish cleaning ceremony takes place. The cleaning board was built onto the south side of the barn and its specifications called for dimensions that would accommodate a seventy-five-pound bass—so far, it has not been tested to its full capacity. A bass is a delightful fish to clean. If he has been wrapped in newspaper and put directly onto the ice in the fish box, he will remain moist. Consequently, the scales are easily stripped off. Then the dorsal and anal fins are ripped out, the ventrals sliced, and the pectorals dissected off. When the fish is gutted, the head and tail cut off, and the remainder split, the backbone can be removed, leaving two fillets of firm flesh containing absolutely no bones except for a few large ribs in the flank. Head and tail are carefully preserved for a future chowder. To-day's fish is a nice little five-pounder and his head will hardly, of itself, do for a chowder, but we ate his twin yesterday and the two heads will be just enough.

While all this has been going on, the womenfolk have been setting the table, preparing potatoes, making cream sauce, and such things. The kettles are singing softly, indicating a good fire, and by the time the fish has been cleaned,

observations made as to sex and latest feeding habits, the fish board swashed off, and so forth, it is almost time to start broiling.

To broil a fish properly, the fire should be burning down. Too hot a fire will burn the flesh before it is cooked. On the other hand, if it is too low, the flesh will get dry. This is quite a delicate point. The other delicate point comes in cooking the fish just the right length of time. There is a very narrow range between not enough cooking, so that the shoulder meat has a slippery, raw look, and too much cooking, so that the flesh is mealy, dry, and tasteless. Frequent turning is, of course, necessary, and I like to do most of the cooking with the skin side down, not worrying if it gets burned.

On do-nothing day, the fish usually comes out pretty well. When he appears on the table, lightly browned, and gently bathed in melted butter with just a touch of lemon juice added, there is no further delay. All hands set to and silence reigns.

With the ending of dinner and the inevitable cleanup afterwards, do-nothing day is about over. A long nap is in order, from which we wake up relaxed and contented. We may take the car to Round Pond to see if it holds any teal, or to catch a glimpse of a deer coming down for a sip of water, or we may drive over to the West Shore to watch the sunset. A light supper of soup, toast, and jam satisfies everybody. Afterwards, a small fire in the fireplace feels pleasant. The northwest wind has died out, the air has a distinct Fall tinge and the stars are very bright and clear.

When we take our last outdoor observation before going

to bed, we find a bright show of northern lights. For a while we stand and watch the shimmering streamers suddenly shoot up toward the zenith and as suddenly disappear. At one end of the arc an orange-yellow color appears, and at the other, over near the house, the color becomes almost blood red.

"Some folks say," Tom, our iceman, once remarked after asking us if we had, the night before, seen the northern lights, "some folks say it means the END."

Well, we begin to shiver, and it means the end of the day for us. One by one, we disappear into our respective bedrooms. The last to go blows out the lamps and stands for a moment before the fireplace, while the flickering light of the dying fire casts an enormous shadow against the ceiling.

Yes, we have all kinds of days here at the Farm House. They are all good, but one of the best is do-nothing day.

10. The West Shore

WHEN I was a boy, I used to spend every Christmas vacation at the Great Pond Camp in Eastham. This camp was very gradually assembled by my father. It started with a small shack to keep warm the gunners who were shooting the "blind," and finally developed into a comfortable, sprawling building, nestled down among black alders and cedars. In the beginning, the gunners would walk over from the Farm House to shoot, and then back again for dinner, but, when I was growing up, the Pond Camp was a going concern, and the little Farm House remained deserted.

At Christmas time, we hoped and prayed for a real nor'-wester. Under such conditions, the black ducks coming out of the Nauset Marsh at Eastham, and Pleasant Bay at Chatham, would cross the Cape in the vicinity of the Great Pond, pitch down over the pines on the northwest shore of the pond, and skim the half mile of dunes to the West Shore at grass-top level. Once in a dog's age, conditions would be just right, and we could station ourselves on the sand hills

overlooking the shore and have the prettiest and most difficult pass shooting that ever was.

All night, through your sleep, you hear the northwest
wind roaring through the cedars and across the wide-angled
roof, rustling and slatting the pine boughs fastened there in
order to hide the house from ducks' sharp eyes. You wonder
if the wind will hold through the morning. Finally the time
comes to get up. After a quick snack, you start on a fumbling
dark walk around the corner of the barn where old Dan'l,
Tom's horse, stamps impatiently, along the weedy shore of
the pond, crisscrossed by narrow trenches where the dogs
have been digging out muskrats, and around the sandy
stretch at the southwest end of the cove, where the bitter
wind bites through your clothing and makes your teeth ache.
The party is led by long-legged Uncle Frank, who takes
a hurried glance over his shoulder at the now brightening
eastern sky, and increases his stride still more. You have to
open your mouth to get more air, and that makes your teeth
ache even more. You breathe a little tune, probably the "Our
Director" march, to keep your legs going fast enough. And
then comes that blessed moment of respite as you enter the
path, an old abandoned road that runs through a quarter
mile of gnarled and ancient pitch pines. The wind roars
overhead, but below all is peace and quiet and warmth. However, your respite is brief, for abruptly you emerge from the
woods, and the wind smites you with increased fury. Up
and down, up and down, you stumble over the frozen surface
of the low dunes. By now the eastern sky shows pink, and
already you have seen a shadowy pair of ducks disappear into
the western gloom.

At last, after what seems a long, long time, but which is only about half an hour, you reach the thirty- to forty-foot cliffs at the edge of the beach. The sea stretches into space, and the white water, as the waves break over the barely covered flats, is now clearly visible. You take your stand a couple of hundred yards from the next man, sit down, preferably in the lee of a beach-plum bush, and face the dawn.

Hardly have you had time to load your gun when you catch sight of three dark shapes silhouetted against the reddening sky. Ducks! They disappear behind the crest of a dune, show for a second as they rise, and disappear again. Will they come close to you? Suddenly they appear right in front of you, rise up a few feet, and then slide slantingly down through a gully. You fire two futile shots as the ducks continue to bore steadily into the wind and finally drop down behind the cliffs. Faint pops on either side indicate that the others are busy too.

And now the flight is really on. There are ducks in the air all the time. They look like bumblebees, you think, as they come straight at you, their round, dark bodies without visible heads and their wings only a blur. Sometimes an unsuspected duck will suddenly pass over, not six feet away, and disappear so quickly that you cannot fire a shot. Your gun barrels begin to get hot, which is good for your hands but not for your temper, for you have not yet bagged a duck. Then along come three. They start to pass to the left, the middle bird well behind and below the leader. You shoot at the leader, and the second bird drops dead. Triumphantly you run out and pick him up. A duck is a duck. Never mind if you have committed the cardinal error—too low and too late.

The sun comes over the pines, dazzling your eyes and adding to your difficulties. The ducks begin to thin out and to fly higher, sometimes out of range. Another hour passes, and only a straggler comes by. Uncle Frank stands up and waves, and you all reassemble and count the score. You have your duck, Uncle Frank has eight, and the others, two or three apiece. Nobody has done really well, except for Uncle Frank, and even he has had his difficulties.

The walk back is easy. The path through the pines is almost too warm now. When you come to the little outlet that runs out of the Great Pond into the Ice Pond, you stop for a moment. A single cock whistler has seen some movement, and makes a fast getaway, the music of his rapidly beating wings plainly audible in spite of the wind. He circles and comes downwind over your head. A barrage of eight shots does him no harm.

Finally you reach camp, and find six-foot pine logs roaring in the fireplace. A second breakfast suddenly appears—cereal and scrambled eggs, sausages and bacon.

"My, I'm stuffed," says George, finally.

"But George," says his mother, "there are griddlecakes coming."

"Well," he replies, nothing daunted, "I've still got my neck!"

It is a longish walk from the Farm House to the West Shore, certainly all of three miles, and we frequently are tempted to take the car, even in spring, when our major activity consists of walking. Sometimes we hike it, passing by to the east and north of the Great Pond, through the pines, and across the dunes to the beach. We come out at the

Herring Brook, which runs out of the Ice Pond, and up which alewives run in the spring, especially if the tiny, foot-wide stream has been cleared of obstructions. This brook runs so straight that it must, many years ago, have been dug for the purpose of taking these herring. Thence we turn south to the "Scene of the First Encounter," the hill that lies between the Great Meadow and the West Shore, where the Pilgrims were said to have had a skirmish with the Indians; and finally home by way of "Widder" Harding's and the Railroad Ponds. All told, it may amount to only an eight- or ten-mile walk, but we are always plenty tired when we get back.

The West Shore beach is composed of very fine, soft sand (let the motorist beware!) and is bordered by a varying amount of salt-water sedge. Beyond the grass, at low water, stretch the flats, away and away, for a mile and a half or more on a really "low dreen." The wise man carries a pocket compass when he goes out on these flats. People have been drowned in the flooding tide when a thick fog has suddenly shut in, causing them to lose their sense of direction. An experienced man should be able to find his way back by noting how lie the little sand riffles, made by the breeze as the tide ebbed off, as well as the direction of the shallow runs that usually make off to the northwest. Even so, a compass is a comfort.

Up until the time of the great eelgrass catastrophe, these sand flats were covered with a thick carpet of short eelgrass. In this grass, large, sharp-edged puddles were formed which might hold a foot or more of water, even at low tide. It was a fascinating pastime, in the summer, to wade through these puddles and to watch the myriad forms of life which they held.

Stand still, knee-deep, in one of them, and wait. Two small hermit crabs appear and soon are engaged in what looks like a life and death struggle. Suddenly, almost faster than the eye can follow, each one whisks out of his own shell and into the other's. In a second they whisk back again. This performance has always reminded me of trying on somebody else's shoes and finding them uncomfortable.

Now suddenly a small area of sand moves, and you discover it is not sand at all, but a two-inch flounder. Something alarms him, and with a slight shake, he buries his body in the sand, leaving uncovered his two tiny, dark eyes. A large sand crab, his back a speckled pink, wanders by and fails to notice the hidden flounder. He does dislodge a shrimp, which backs off in a series of jerks and is immediately pursued by a very large minnow. The flounder would have made a pass at the shrimp had he known of the shrimp's presence, and the crab would have done the same to the flounder. And as for the crab, let him look out for the great black-backed gull yonder. That heavy bill bodes ill.

We never knew what might turn up next in one of these puddles, and time passed rapidly. The sudden realization that the flood tide had started to float the eelgrass always gave us a shock of surprise.

In the late summer, one of our favorite expeditions was going out with Francis to tend his traps. These were of the weir type, constructed of netting hung on poles, the latter having been sunk deep into the sand by the simple expedient of pumping a stream of water down along the base of the pole. This stream would soon soften the sand into a deep hole, and it was always surprising to see how rapidly the pole would sink to a depth of four feet or more. A long "stringer" or "leader" led offshore to the trap proper, which was placed near the edge of the low-water mark. The stringer led into the "heart"—named because of its shape—at the apex of which was a narrow opening with doors swinging inward, leading to an enclosure about forty feet in diameter. Sometimes this was shaped so as to lead to still another, smaller enclosure with a small conical aperture similar to, though larger than, that seen in an eel trap or lobster pot. Fish traveling alongshore strike the leader, run out along it to the heart and so into the trap. The trouble was, the striped bass seemed always to be too smart. Even in those years, when acres of them could be seen almost any day near the shore, seldom did more than a few of them get fooled by the maze. These traps did not often make much money. I think it was more the fascination of the chase, the anticipatory excitement of wading offshore and wondering if *today* might be the big day, that kept Francis at it.

I have been out there with him when a stiff northeast wind drove the rain through your clothing, and wading in the cold water made you shiver. But the best time to go out is on a warm, sunny morning. You arrive at "The First Encounter" about ten o'clock, just as the water is dropping off the flats. The sky is clear, the sun bright and warm. Off to the northwest, the remnants of that sandy island once known as Billingsgate—where, as a boy, I used to shoot shore birds—looms up in a wavy mirage. The Dennis shore is sharp and clear, while almost due west, a bit of land is just visible, the heights of Manomet.

The flats are dotted with shore birds, mostly sanderling and black-bellied plover, with here and there a flock of scattered yellowlegs searching the puddles.

As we approach the heart of the trap, the water deepens until it nearly reaches our knees. Excitement becomes intense. What manner of fish shall we see today? The urge is to hurry, but the deep water and the necessity for inspecting the bottom, especially for hidden crabs, before putting down a bare foot, makes progress slow. Finally we reach the gate and peer inside. There is a flurry of water within the enclosure, but we cannot make out what it denotes, so we slip in and close the gate behind us.

The first thing we see then is a high dorsal fin slowly moving through the water. Dogfish? Or shark? Somehow bare feet do not seem so desirable now. The fin turns out to belong to a toothless dogfish, and we feel reassured. Sometimes fair-sized sharks get into the trap, but I have never heard of anyone being hurt by them.

Suddenly a school of tinker mackerel dart by. They remind me of tigers, the almost vertical dark stripes on their backs contrasting sharply with the lighter areas. They are really stunning in the bright light, as all together they turn this way and that, and cast their shadows against the yellow sand. Three small two-pound bluefish flash by with amazing speed, and disappear toward the farther end as they search for a non-existent outlet. Four or five good-sized kingfish (the ground kingfish, not the Spanish mackerel) hug the bottom of the net, and the V-shaped stripes on their backs, alternating dark and light, make a striking pattern. A school of large pogies are making a great fuss at one end of the trap, while a compact bunch of six-inch squid dart hither and yon, propelling themselves first forwards and then backwards with equal facility. In case you do not know it, they are the precursor of the jet-propelled plane, only the latter has not yet learned to fly backwards. Occasionally, if too much alarmed, squid will emit an inky cloud, this being their only method of protection aside from their speed. It has always seemed to me that they travel faster backwards than forwards.

Gingerly, you take a few steps out toward the center. Huge spider crabs, a foot or more in diameter, make any rapid progress seem undesirable, although these crabs are relatively harmless as crabs go. Suddenly there is a great upheaval, as the bottom goes out from under you. You have stepped on a plaice-fish, or summer flounder, which had buried itself in the sand. To step with bare feet on a small flounder is disconcerting, to say the least, but to step on an eight-pound plaice-fish is a devastating experience.

By now the situation has been fairly well sized up. There are not enough marketable fish to make it worth while to get out the seine. With stout-handled, large-mouthed nets, we proceed to try to dip out the few desirable fish there are. Francis uses the "bashing" technique, by which he stuns a fish so that it may be captured. The rest of us use the "herd in a corner and dip" technique. The former method is good for bass and weakfish, the latter for kingfish and plaice. No technique is very successful for bluefish. We have a merry time trying to catch the bluefish, but when finally the flooding tide makes further netting impossible, there is still one bluefish left, his speed undiminished as he whirls around the trap edge. We leave him, hoping that he will attract many more on the next high tide.

Francis spends the last few available minutes mending the netting, where heaving waves have torn the weed-laden line. Sometimes, if a heavy storm comes when there is a lot of weed in the water, it may take a week or more to repair the damage, even when, with the aid of lights, night tides are utilized. It seems like heartbreaking work, and the wonder is that any one is willing to put up with all the trials and tribulations involved in it. And yet, and yet, the thrill is there—the thrill of the hunt, of the chase; the desire to outwit your adversary, the satisfaction of having built with your own hands, and planned with your own strategy. It is every bit as real as the satisfaction the purest of dry-fly fishermen gets when, with the most delicate technique, he lands a half-pound trout. And the trap fisherman has always an added excitement which the fly fisherman has not, because the trap's success may mean bread and butter for its owner. If he likes fish, so long as the trap is in operation, he will not starve.

Some day, say in late October, drive over to the West Shore just at sundown. The breeze has died out flat, the sky is cloudless, the tide is at full flood. Square offshore, the crimson sun is sliding with surprising rapidity into a tranquil sea. A hardy flock of black-bellied plover flash by, chuckling softly to themselves as they head for their roost on Jeremy Point. Heavy-flying herring gulls, no longer able to take advantage of the breeze, seem to bounce up and down as they, too, make for their customary sleeping place. As you look at the sun with your bird glasses, you can see across the face of it several small, ragged, dark spots—the sunspots about which so much is written and so little known. And now, if you will, you may obtain a rather frightening impression of the earth's rotation. Think of yourself as a very small spot on the curved surface of the earth. You know it is curved, because, as you gaze across the water, it looks that way. Imagine that you are whirling around, away from the sun. Look once, look away, and look back—already the sun is half hidden. Look away, and back again—a quarter left. Away, and back—only a tiny rim. Away and back again—the sun has gone, and you must whirl for nearly another twelve hours before you will meet it again coming up out of the ocean.

Suddenly the air feels cold, and you, very insignificant. As you turn back toward the car, the measured cadence of a hooting horned owl booms out of the woods.

"Who? Who, Who-oo? Who? Who?" he asks.

Who indeed?

11. Eelgrass and Depressions

"YOU mean to say that economic booms and depressions are due to emotional factors?" My younger colleague was horrified. Unlike most medical men, he had a firm grasp of the theory of economics and financial problems in general. In addition, he held what might be called quite radical views concerning our social setup. He had been talking very interestingly about national and international finance—the gold standard, debtor and creditor nations, and so forth—and obviously was much upset at my remark. But in spite of a somewhat malicious desire to mix my friend up, I did indeed have a definite feeling that he was making rules and drawing conclusions from an uncertain source—uncertain, because it depended on mass emotion.

To me it seems clear that there is a rhythmic variation in the mass emotion of human beings. For a period, there is a gradually increasing manic phase, which, at its peak, and seen in the light of a more normal period, is nothing short of "craziness," a mass psychosis. Comes the crash, and, as in individuals suffering from a similar disease, the manic phase suddenly shifts to one of depression.

In terms of economics, the manic phase is accompanied by a buying compulsion. Any scarce item will be bought at high prices and sold for still higher prices. People will rush to buy land many feet under water and pay fabulous prices therefor. The value of the dollar drops, prices and wages rise, and the inflation wheel spins faster and faster until the crash comes. The sudden depressive phase results in just the opposite. Nobody buys anything that is not absolutely essential. Money is hoarded, prices and wages drop, unemployment increases.

Gold is only valuable because man thinks it is. Money is worthless if people suddenly decide they will not play that game any more. As soon as one person begins to question the value of money, the crowd follows. Panic ensues.

Thus I say that booms and depressions are fundamentally biological in their development. The financial and mathematical method of approach is simply a way of describing the effects of these biological changes. I do not mean to decry such methods, for they help us to understand the situation, and may lead to methods effective in cushioning the force of the reaction. Fundamentally, the cure must lie in discovering the biological cause, and either preventing or treating it.

I believe this biological effect is the human counterpart of cycles seen in many lower animals, in this case expressed in terms of abundance or scarcity.

Take, for instance, the lemming cycle. This is approximately a ten-year cycle, during which these rodents rapidly increase until they reach a period of tremendous abundance. Then, suddenly, something happens, and in two years they have practically disappeared. The ecological effect of this sudden disappearance is vast. The arctic foxes, who have also increased, largely due to this source of abundant food, are suddenly left starving, and they greatly decrease in numbers. The snowy owls no longer find their lemmings, the sick foxes give out, and consequently these birds spread out all over the Northern Hemisphere looking for food. The next time you see a snowy owl slowly turning his knob-like head to keep his glowing yellow eye fixed on yours, you will know there is a lemming depression in the north.

The question is, is this lemming cycle in any way connected with human cycles? I have never seen boom peaks or depression valleys plotted against the years of snowy owl abundance in New England. I would not expect them to correlate absolutely, even if there were some relation, for there must be many other factors, and it is probable that all factors must point more or less in the same direction before a boom or depression becomes apparent.

In searching for a fundamental cause of these biological cycles, one must turn to some factor involving the source of this earth's energy. In spite of all the jokes about it, I still think that periods of sunspot maxima may well be definitely related to these cycles. Sunspots are known to be evidence of greatly increased outbursts of energy at the solar surface. They are known to be related to other phenomena such as electric "storms" and auroral displays. There is some evidence that the total radiation to the earth in the form of heat is increased during these maxima. I am not saying that sunspot maxima will necessarily coincide with the financial cycles described above; I do imply that financial crises are brought about by some change in the earth's supply of energy.

Perhaps if we knew why the eelgrass suddenly left the

Northern Atlantic area, we might have the answer. In 1907 the Nauset Marsh was lush with eelgrass. I can remember too well when I was a boy trying to help my brother-in-law push a boat through the mud-embedded grass. In 1912 it was practically all gone; in 1919 it started coming back; and by 1922 the marsh was full of it. However, in 1928 it began to disappear again, and by 1932 it had completely disappeared. This time it went, not only locally, but from every part of the coast supplied by the North Atlantic Ocean, European as well as American. Today, 1946, it is coming in again, not only in the Nauset Marsh but also in many other areas. Is it of significance that both world wars occurred during periods of eelgrass dearth?

The total effect of eelgrass disappearance is quite astonishing. Of course the conchologists get depressed because eelgrass patches are their great hunting ground. Black ducks, which feed in, if not on, the eelgrass, become at least locally scarce, and hunters get grumpy and ill-tempered. Brant, which feed *on* eelgrass, become nearly extinct, and the cook and guides at the "X" Club are out of a job. Scallops, no longer able to hide, rapidly disappear, thus ruining a thriving business in such places as Marion, on Buzzards Bay. Clams cannot get seeded, and the clam industry is cleaned out. And outboard motorboats can go thundering all over the place, driving all peace-loving residents crazy.

The cause of the disappearance has not been too clearly established. Those theories having to do with the salinity of the water, hard winters, and so forth, were obviously not correct. It seems pretty certain that the eelgrass was killed by a certain fungus, but why the grass suddenly became susceptible, or the fungus vicious, has not been clarified. Is there some relationship to the life cycles of birds and mammals?

When I had finished my discourse, and had managed to link booms and depressions to the cyclic variations of lemming abundance, the southern winter wanderings of snowy owls, and the disappearance of eelgrass from the Atlantic coasts, my financial friend looked at me for a full minute without speaking. Then he shook his head, and abruptly left the table.

12. Beach and Sea

FROM the Farm House we can look over the hill and across the Nauset Marsh to the dunes, and beyond them, where they are low or have become hollowed out, to the sea. Sometimes its color is bright blue, sometimes green, sometimes gray. Not infrequently a fog bank, lying offshore like a huge rolled-up carpet, will suddenly begin to unroll itself and to blot out sea and dunes alike. However, really to get the feel of the sea, to know its whims and caprices, its gentleness and its fury, you have to be right there, in it or by it.

The sea's moods are never the same. They may, and usually do, change with startling rapidity. Better to be standing on the beach than to be out in a flimsy boat, if the sea's anger is suddenly aroused. Even then, you may be in trouble.

Pitted against the vast ocean, which, unhindered, stretches off to the east and around the earth's curve to the coast of Spain, is the Nauset Beach, the Great Beach. From the tip of Monomoy, for forty miles it runs almost due north, unbroken except for narrow inlets into Pleasant Bay at Chatham and the Nauset Marsh at Eastham. North of the Coast Guard Station, it is bordered by relatively high cliffs, while to the south the only barrier to the marsh is a line of sand dunes, some low, some high. Peculiarly enough, however, the cliffs seem to be the most vulnerable. Within my memory, the old Nauset Lifesaving Station had to be abandoned, and on a hill two hundred yards to the rear the new Coast Guard Station was built. The old station toppled into the sea before all the material in it could be salvaged. This means that I have seen the ocean eat into the land at least one hundred and twenty feet during the past forty years.

Not so the dunes. Houses are built along the dune beach and houses are washed away; dunes grow big and then disappear; the hundred-yard-wide strip of land is cut through in big storms and high tides, and sand comes spreading over the marsh grass; but the cut is soon plugged again, and the marsh remains undisturbed. What the sea takes from one spot it builds up in another, and each year the piping plover must hunt for a low, beach-grass-covered rise of just the right height for a nest. The dune beach, though its contours are ever changing, remains unbroken, its defenses intact.

The sea is never quiet. Even when it is at its most serene, there comes from it a continuous low hum, or murmur, which waxes and wanes, and out of which arise a lot of little sounds. Voices do not carry far at the sea's edge, no matter how calm it may be. Secrets, if you must have them, can here be spoken aloud, for voices will not be heard except at very close range.

I remember one September night, fishing the beach by moonlight. We arrived about ten o'clock with the tide at half flood and the moon high and full. There was not a breath of air and the ocean was as calm as I have ever seen it. Even then, however, there was a slight uneasiness about it, a gentle heave and thrust, that caused small waves to tumble against the beach and send a whispering cadence back to the dunes.

It seemed as bright as day as we somewhat gingerly waded into the cold water and began to cast. Tight riffles, made by schools of bait, appeared at the edge of the shelf. Soon bass began to break water in the midst of these schools, but the familiar pistol-shot sound of their feeding, which we frequently hear in the marsh, was so muffled by the sea's quiet voice as to be almost inaudible. As is usual when we get excited, our casting immediately began to suffer, and backlashes appeared. The bass would chase the bait right up onto the beach at our feet, not four paces away. I hooked one with only a rod's length of line out. The fish grabbed my eel and started off with a tremendous burst of speed. The whirling reel handle caught my thumb before I could get it out of the way, and for several days a very painful thumb it was.

We caught three bass in short order, all small—that is, five to seven pounds—and then they stopped biting. We fished right over the high water without any more excitement until well after four o'clock, when the moon already was becoming orange-tinted. And all this time, not the slightest riffle disturbed the glassy calmness of the sea. It seemed almost as if we were fishing from the shore of the Salt Pond.

Some day, try casting with your surf outfit into the Salt Pond. You take your stance at the edge of the pond and make your whiplike cast. The rod, as it snaps through the air, produces a swishing sound, the reel spool utters a loud whirring noise, somewhat resembling an old and rickety electric fan, and the bait hits the water with an immense splash that will frighten any bass within a hundred yards.

Take the same cast on the beach, however, no matter how calm the sea, and you do not hear a sound. When the bait hits the water, there is a splash, to be sure, clearly visible in the bright moonlight, but it makes no noise, and probably only serves to attract the attention of any nearby bass.

No, even at its quietest, most docile moments, the sea is a trifle restless, its immense energy only reluctantly restrained. Standing knee-deep in water, halfway down the rise, you do not need to keep a watchful eye lest the next oncoming wave give you a wetting. But the power is there; you can feel it, as gentle currents play about your feet.

Tonight all is peace and quiet; watch out for tomorrow.

Sometimes we find the sea in a joyous mood. I well remember a day in early November. There was a brisk northwest breeze, a remnant of the previous day's nor'wester that had cleared away an easterly storm. The blue sky was filled with small, broken cumulus clouds, which hurried across the Cape as if on their way to some important rendezvous at sea. The air was clear and sparkling, and just cold enough to give us the energy needed for our beach walk.

The marsh was full of black ducks. When we came by the Goose Hummocks—or by the site of the Goose Hummocks, for they long since have been washed away—we started at least five hundred ducks off the flats. Flocks of sheldrake (red-breasted mergansers), interspersed with a few early whistlers, were trading up and down the channel. On the flats, bunches of red-backed sandpipers were scattered about. A few late black-bellied plovers, running fast and stopping suddenly, were stoking up preparatory to taking a long journey. We guessed their intentions by noting their constant calling, knowing that on such a day they are likely to start off for warmer climates. It was not until we rounded the point of the beach at the Inlet, however, that we really felt the joy of the sea.

The tide on the outside was at half flood, and already the outer bars were well under water. The northwest breeze had kicked up quite a chop through which moderate easterly seas, generated by the recent storm, were still rolling in to the beach. The ocean was a brittle blue, speckled here and there with whitecaps, especially offshore, far from the lee of the dunes. The choppy waves, riffled by the wind, danced gaily along, apparently bedecked with bright jewels which glinted and shone in the sunlight.

Meanwhile the surf kept pounding steadily in against the breeze, the crest of each wave plumed with a white streamer which drifted off to leeward. The bigger waves were breaking mostly on the outer bars, but smaller secondary waves came prancing up to the beach and fell with happy abandon at our feet.

There was a constant stream of fowl flying south, some low, some high. Long lines of eiders, the males a stunning contrast in black and white, passed by, barely skimming the surface of the water and often disappearing behind a wave crest. Loose bunches of coot—mostly white-wings, flying fairly high—came hurtling by, their heavy bodies propelled by their relatively small wings at an incredibly rapid rate. A flock of loons—the big loons—came along, also headed south. A flock may consist of eight or ten loons, each separated from the next by at least three or four hundred yards. In the daytime they can maintain liaison by sight. I have never heard them talking to each other, at least to recognize it. Perhaps at night they close ranks.

Occasional flocks of black ducks came in straight from the east, boring steadily into the wind until they had crossed the dune strip, and pitched down to meet their brethren in back of Teal Hummock. Several skeins of geese, most of them in an unusually unkempt formation, drifted down along the shore, crossed the dunes a short distance above the Inlet, and, steadily gaining height as well as order, disappeared to the southwest.

The beach itself seemed nearly white and was almost

overpoweringly bright. We had to squint when we looked toward the north to see if the old wreck by the Beach House had come out again. We found that it had, after having been buried for two years, and when we came up to it, we sat for a while on one of the big timbers, wondering what had been the fate of this once staunch ship.

Finally we made our way back to the Coast Guard Station and the car. Our spirits were light, our minds free, and a mild joke was unusually happily received. Why not? The sea was in a happy mood and so were we.

In its regal mood, the sea is superb. This is most likely to occur during the hurricane season, in August or September. The storm need not be experienced ashore. Generally, no report of a storm is available, though possibly if one perused the shipping news one might find reference to some severe storm at sea. Such a storm, originating, say in the Caribbean region, may pass by many hundreds of miles offshore and create huge waves which, unhindered, roll on and on, finally to crash with a thundering roar on the Nauset Beach.

From the Farm House platform, when we take our morning observation, we see long rollers coming in through the Inlet on the flood tide. Every once in a while a column of ocean spray, gleaming in the bright sunlight, rises straight up into the air above all but the highest dunes. In spite of a fresh westerly breeze, the roar of the surf a mile away comes plainly to us, now suddenly loud from the northeast, now from the southeast.

From the bluff at the Coast Guard Station, we have a magnificent view. Wave after wave, in stately majesty, comes rolling slowly and irresistibly toward the shore. On the outer bar the water piles up in a veritable mountain, and, as the crest topples over in a mass of white foam, the illusion of a snow-capped mountain peak becomes even more striking. As the water shoals up, steeper and higher become the waves. Their backs begin to hump up and curve away in an easy slope to the following trough, while the forward wall becomes more and more concave. Eagerly, the top of the wave rushes on while the foot, in its struggle with the friction of the sandy bottom, is more and more slowed up. The suspense is almost unbearable, as for one breath-taking moment the wave seems to hang in mid-air. Then comes a deafening crash, which shakes the beach, and a smother of white foam leaps high into the sky as if to snatch at the sun.

Take out your watch and time the interval between crests. Eleven seconds? Twelve seconds? Even thirteen? No ordinary storm built such waves as these! Such a storm must have been of real hurricane proportions.

There is a good panoramic view from the bluff, but to get the real feel of the sea, you must be down on the beach. Watch out, though; the tide is rising, and already some of those thunderous waves are eating away the steep face of the dunes. From the beach you do not have the same perspective, and the immense size of the waves becomes very much more apparent. As you stand near the top of the rising, so high is the oncoming wave that it seems to tower over your head. The roar is intensified, a constant, all-pervading din, interrupted only by the louder crash of each succeeding wave. Conversation is impossible. A few words, shouted into the ear, are as much as you can manage. And along the beach, the sunlight is diffused into a halo effect by a fine fog of spray.

Try now to figure which are destined to be the bigger waves and which the smaller. From above this seemed relatively easy; from below it becomes a thousand times more difficult. It has been said that every seventh wave will be a big one, but this has not been my experience. There seems to be a certain rhythm, it is true, and big waves do tend to come in threes, but the rhythm is not dependable, at least not sufficiently so to count on it if you have to launch a lifeboat. Even so, if you have great patience, there will always come a time when the seas are relatively small. Take her out then, if you must; take her out surely and quickly, and never, never think of turning back. Likely you will have to climb up over a steep mountain of water, and you may smash down so hard in the next trough that the bow goes clean under, but if you have figured correctly, and if you keep heading out, you will make it.

Then how about coming in? If it was a thousand times harder from the beach than from the bluff to predict the seas, it is still another thousand times more difficult when you are actually at sea. I know, because I have been there.

Many years ago, a couple of friends and I elected to row a sort of half dory from Scituate to the Duxbury Beach. Not until after we were out in it did we realize that there was a tremendous surf—the longest and biggest, we found out afterwards, that had been seen in years. Being young and stubborn, we continued on our way. Loaded down with duffel, we could not keep too far offshore, because the fresh southwest breeze would then begin to slop water aboard; nor could we come in too close and risk being caught by a breaking sea. Once, we decided to pass inside a shoal which lay about half a mile offshore. I shall never forget that tense moment when, just as we came abreast of it, a huge wave began to mount higher and higher. Fortunately for us, the wave did not topple, and the danger, for the moment, was over.

However, at Brant Rock Point we gave up. Beyond the point, the southwest chop was too much for us. We chose a spot directly opposite what was then the Brant Rock Life-saving Station, and began to edge in toward shore. Just here the difficulty began. At what spot were the waves, on the average, beginning to break? If you knew, you could come up close to that spot, wait for a series of small waves, and follow in behind one of them as fast as you could row, in order to get in before the next big one came along. This sounds very well on paper, but it did not seem so easy as we lay on our oars and watched the great waves thunder in to the beach.

At this point, one of the lifesaving crew waved a red flag, and we hung off. In what seemed like a very short space of time, the lifeboat, not then motorized, was negotiated out through the surf and came alongside. We transferred our gear and ourselves, and cast the dory adrift. The Captain put us amidships and then very slowly began to creep in-shore, keeping his head turned over his shoulder as he tried to gauge the weight of the oncoming waves.

For a long time, we lay there, fully fifteen minutes I should think, when suddenly he cried, "Now!"

The boat came to life as the crew bent to their oars. Then ominously a wave, smaller than most, to be sure, rose higher and higher astern. The lifeboat came up on the wave's crest, and, gathering speed, slowly started to point her bow downward. All at once she began to yaw to port.

The Captain, with his steering oar over the starboard quarter, put all his weight on it, but could not straighten us out. Quick as a flash, the stroke oarsman jerked his oar out of the lock and slid it over the same quarter. This proved to be just enough to bring us around, and we shot in, riding the wave, at what seemed to me the speed of light.

I do not know how close a call this was. From what little experience I have had, I should say it was too close, for had we yawed around just a little further, nothing on earth could have stopped us. In a jiffy we would have turned broadside to the sea, and been rolled over and over like a bobbin on a spinning machine. As it was, we landed gently on the beach. Quickly we hopped out, very thankful to feel terra firma beneath us, while the crew heaved the boat up out of reach of the next wave.

I have heard it said that, if one is in a Banks fishing dory, and must come in through a heavy surf, the thing to do is to lie down in the eyes of her and wait. The dory is supposed always to come ashore, upright and dry. However this may be, when finally we looked around for our abandoned boat, we were astonished to find her right side up on the beach. We looked inside, and there was not a drop of water in her.

Yes, when the sea is in a regal mood, it is wonderful to watch it from bluff or beach. But my advice would be to remain there, or possibly, if one is not subject to seasickness, to stay far offshore. Anything in between means trouble, bad trouble.

Sometimes the sea becomes furiously angry. At the Farm House we awaken, on an April day, to find the wind blowing straight out from the northeast and driving rain before it. On such a day, anyone with any sense would "hole in" and spend the day on household tasks, or read, or play cribbage. The "cabinet" might well be rearranged and made shipshape. This "cabinet" is a closet, situated beside the fireplace. Its many shelves hold all manner of junk, so that rarely does the tinkerer fail to find whatever he needs, provided he has the time and the patience to look for it.

Instead of doing this, however, we are likely for some strange reason to take the car and drive to the Coast Guard Station. As we get out, for the first time we feel the full force of the gale. A fine, driving rain, mixed with sand and salt spray, stings our faces as we try to look into it. The sky is a sullen gray, with low and wispy clouds racing by overhead. Visibility is limited to about one mile. The sea, too, is gray, a livid and threatening gray. There are no long, heavy waves now. All is a jumbled mass of gray and white water. Short, steep waves tumble this way and that, jostle and thump each other, tear and bite at the beach, and spit out spume that rises over the bluff and trails off to leeward. And from it comes a steady, deafening roar, augmented by the roar of the wind which sucks at our clothing as if to rip it off.

Once a man stood near us on the bluff, his slicker flapping and slatting like a blown-out spinnaker. He was holding a big graflex camera. First he would turn into the storm and look into his finder. Then he would turn back, take out a handkerchief, and wipe off the lens. After repeating this process several times, he looked up at us with a woebegone expression and yelled something which we could not hear.

I came closer and cupped my hand to my ear. "I like *fresh* water best!" he shouted.

We do not stay long here, and soon start our walk down the beach. Of course, we follow the inside or marsh edge of the dunes, where there is a little lee. The walk down is deceptively easy with the wind and rain at our backs, and we must be careful not to go too far. As a rule the walk is uneventful. Black ducks, for instance, in such weather pod down in some protected spot and stay there. A few horned larks will start up at our feet and drift rapidly off to leeward, uttering their thin little squeak, and very possibly a flock of early winter yellowlegs, all facing to windward, may be seen huddled up in the marsh grass.

When we come to the cut-through above the Beach House, we cross over to the outer beach and out to the top of the rising. Here the anger of the sea seems even more vicious, and the noises more deafening. Already, due to an unusually high run of tides, the wash is coming up over the rising and spilling down the cut-through. As one stands there in the roar and tumult, leaning against the gale and trying to look into it, one feels singularly helpless. This is surely no place for a fisherman, whether he be afoot or asea.

Even though we again take the inside route, the walk back is a tough, unpleasant grind. We bend low, keep our faces down, and buck into the wind. After what seems like a long time, we reach the road and the car, and when the motor responds to the starter with a steady purr, all hands heave a great sigh of relief.

We are once more indoors, fires are stoked, the kitchen becomes festooned with all manner of wet clothing, and warming drinks are prepared. Dressed in dry clothes, and with a hot fire going, we hear the rain slat against the windows as the wind hauls to the south. Now we can contemplate household tasks—cribbage, reading, or even cleaning the cabinet The rest of this day belongs to the Farm House.

13. *Around the Horn*

THE Nauset Marsh at Eastham is an unusual salt marsh. Most such marshes are protected to the seaward by a barrier beach through which an estuary enters. This estuary is widest at its mouth, and divides into smaller and smaller branches which lead into denser and denser bodies of solid sedge.

Not so the Nauset Marsh. It contains more water than sedge and has large bays at the upper end. Even the Main Channel, while nearly two miles from the Inlet, is a quarter of a mile wide. (The Inlet is the passage through the barrier beach.) The sedge is divided into sections. A large one is called "flat" or "marsh," and a small one "hummock." The largest such piece, Porchy Marsh, is about a mile and a half from north to south. Its nearest, or north, edge is about a mile from the Farm House, and the south end about two and a half miles. We call the southernmost tip Cape Horn, and the shallow passageway that makes a tiny island of it, the Straits of Magellan.

One of our best expeditions is "rounding the Horn" in the canoe. To do this, conditions must be just right. In the first place, there must not be so much wind that paddling becomes a task. In the second place, the tide must serve in such a manner that we can drop down the Main Channel on the ebb, meet the flood at the Horn, come up with it, and get home at a comfortable hour for dinner.

It is not too often that all these factors are combined on the same day, so that "rounding the Horn" is a rather infrequent occurrence. And besides all this, let it be said that it requires an expert knowledge of the vagaries of Nauset Marsh tides, as well as a good guess, to hit the "furthest south" at exactly the right moment. Even at best, we are likely to get stuck on the flats below our hill on the way up and have to wait for them to be flooded.

The tide comes right for us this time on the ninth of October. There is a light breeze from the northeast and the air is clean and fresh. From the Farm House piazza the water in the marsh channels is a clear blue, while through the dips in the dunes we can see the deeper blue of the Atlantic Ocean.

As we leave the mouth of the Salt Pond Creek and begin to negotiate the twists and turns of the upper channels, we see many ducks which are strung all the way along the edge of Tom Doane's Hummock. Most of them are black ducks, although we note two hen mallards, one pintail, and perhaps half a dozen baldpates. As we approach, the black ducks begin to take notice. Their necks become straight, long, and stiff, at least twice as long as a duck's neck should be. The nearer ones separate from one another and luff up into the wind, a sure sign that they are about to fly. And off they go, with that spectacular jump of theirs. They drag off others which are not so close, and these in turn drag off others, until at last the whole caboodle is in the air in a great, straggling, lacy flock. Most of them go off straight to the eastward out across the dunes to the ocean, where presumably they will spend the rest of the day asleep.

We soon come to that deep part of the channel, south of the Cedar Bank, where we put out a bucktail fly and begin trolling with our fly rod. This is simply to protect ourselves; for what with the bright sun and very low water, it does not seem like a good chance. The flats are pretty well covered with shore birds. "Winter" yellowlegs and black-bellied plover represent the larger birds, while the smaller ones consist mostly of thousands of red-backed sandpipers. Then suddenly we hear their shrill alarm note and at once every bird is in the air.

"Must be a duck hawk around," I observe.

My wife, in some alarm, snatches off her white hat. A day or two before, when she was sketching, a duck hawk had come along. She had taken up her binoculars and, just as she had them focussed on the hawk, he had made a pass at her hat. This, as seen through her glasses, had been truly terrifying.

"Leave it on," I suggest. "You may attract him."

"Here," she says, "you wear it."

"I guess I won't," I reply.

White hat or no white hat, a handsome full-plumaged male duck hawk comes directly over our heads. Soon he begins to soar and in an incredibly short time has disappeared to the northeast.

And it is just at this point that five huge shore birds come low over our heads and light on the flat in front of us. A quick glance through the glasses shows that they are all godwits, four marbled and one Hudsonian. We all have a good look at these magnificent birds, the largest of all our shore birds. We take a chance on reeling in our line, but the sound does not seem to disturb them. Then we let the canoe drift up toward them.

Three of the marbled godwits are large, and one is considerably smaller. And, as is the case with many nations as well as humans, the larger ones are all picking on the small one. Every time he digs a succulent worm from the ooze, the others go for him, and then what a racket there ensues! I have never heard anything quite like it. It is a sort of cross between Gabriel blowing his horn and the cackling of a hen after she has laid an egg: "*Too*-kity, *Yoo*-kity, Yook!"

We drift up to within thirty feet of them and they don't fly. The marbled godwits show at the base of their long, up-turned bills an orange tinge which we have never noticed before. The Hudsonian is considerably darker and there is a bit of the white patch at the base of his tail which is so obvious when he flies. We leave them to their bickerings and their worms as the ebb takes us slowly past.

We go on down past Hay Island, where some bass boil ahead of the canoe and corroborate the old adage that "A boiling bass never bites." Past the mouth of Jeremiah's Creek, where we put a night heron in a dither as to whether or not to fly. Past the outermost end of Porchy Bar, which so many neophytes have tried to cheat by cutting across too soon, only to find themselves hopelessly stuck on the sand riffles. Past Broad Creek, now, at low water, almost dry except for a few deep holes here and there. Past Deep Water Point, which is no longer a point and where there is no deep water. And finally, down to the sand bar to the south of the Horn.

We see that this sand bar is covered with herring gulls, perhaps two hundred of them, and we wonder why they are standing so still and so erect with all eyes turned in the same direction. There is not a gull in the air and no sound comes from them. And then the reason for this rapt attention becomes apparent.

At the upper end of the bar, austerely aloof, is a large brown bird, about as big as the gulls. When we get the glasses focussed on him, we realize he is a brown gyrfalcon. He seems to be eyeing the gulls with a malevolent expression. As we approach, he turns his baleful eye on us, as if to say: "Get the hell out of here."

But it is he at last who moves. He allows us to come within about fifty yards and finally takes off. As he does so, every gull turns and faces him. He flies directly over them and makes several dives at them. Each time, the target gull spreads his wings, opens his beak wide and screams. And each time, the gyrfalcon swoops up, inches from the gull's head, without touching him.

The gyrfalcon does this about three times and then, off to the east, he spies a marsh hawk. He dashes away and comes down on the marsh hawk from above. But just before he gets there, the marsh hawk flips over on his back, with upraised talons, and again the gyrfalcon swoops up and away. Time after time this performance is repeated, until finally the gyrfalcon tires of the sport and lazily flies away to the

south. In fact, what with his lazy flight and his overall brown color, one could almost mistake him for a year-old herring gull.

I have been diffident about reporting gyrfalcons. These birds have been considered to be exceedingly rare, if not of accidental occurrence, in Massachusetts. If one tells of seeing a gyrfalcon, one can almost hear the unspoken thought, "Probably was a duck hawk." However this may be, I am convinced that gyrfalcons appear regularly on outer Cape Cod. Ever since 1948, when, from October to June, I kept running across the one I wrote about in "Gyrfalcon Pays a Visit," I have seen them at least once a year, usually in October. This is the month when we see the greatest number of duck hawks, and skeptics will make the most of this point.

After this excitement, we go ashore at the end of the sand flat for a stroll and to wait for the flood tide to take hold. We succeed where the gyrfalcon failed—that is, all the gulls take off and begin making slow circles in the air. We walk barefoot over the riffled sand, looking for items of interest, but we find nothing more unusual than that savage shellfish, *Polynices heros*. He is the common big round "snail" which makes a trail in the sand, ending in a very suggestive hump. He is equipped not only with a powerful foot but with an effective rasp as well. He it is who destroys so many mollusks, and he who fashions that smooth sand collar which never meets in the middle, and which holds many thousands of polynices eggs.

When we went ashore, the tide was rising on the flats while still ebbing in the channels. This is a peculiarity of estuaries which is not too difficult to understand. One can see how the water, while still running out of the estuary system, must meet the flow from the sea. In the resulting struggle, the water may, and generally does, rise while it is still flowing out. After about twenty minutes or so, in the Nauset Marsh, the current will coincide with the rise.

But it is rather more difficult to visualize the reverse process. The tide will generally start to fall even while it is still flooding. And this brings up a very curious situation. At the mouth of the estuary the tide will be ebbing and falling, and, at the head, flooding and rising. What happens at that critical point in the middle? It would seem as if the two parts of the watershed must separate and leave a dry place in between. Of course, no such thing occurs. I have been much puzzled by this matter, but I have taken comfort in finding that Hilaire Belloc reports, in *The Cruise of the Nona*, his own mystification.

At any rate, when we climb back into the canoe the tide is flooding strongly. We make our southing and turn with the tide, leaving Cape Horn to starboard. The channel takes us close to the Tonset Shore where eelgrass, the kind that is five or six feet long, has come in thick. We skirt the edge of it and are just approaching the rocks when suddenly the rod man's reel begins to screech.

I back water sharply to stop the canoe's progress, but the fish continues to tear off line. Not only that, but he starts weaving around some lobster buoys which are always to be found in this region. I do my best, in the strong current, to weave the canoe around after him, and must confess to a feeling of relief when he suddenly kicks off.

At this moment someone spies a large white object in the Skiff Hill pastures a quarter of a mile ahead. Various suggestions as to its identity are made, such as a white parasol, an inflated laundry bag, a small tent.

"It's a mushroom," say I, by way of a joke.

At the foot of the pastures we land and climb the green slope. And a mushroom it is! Nine and one-half inches across the top it measures, with a stem an inch and three quarters thick. In the old Farm House log my father wrote of mushrooms as big as dinner plates. Well, this pasture is full of dinner plates and we pick a mess of them to bring home.

These mushrooms, we find later, are not the common field mushroom, *Campestris agaricus,* but a close relative, *Campestris arvensis* or horse mushroom. They are as good to eat if not better, than their smaller cousin. The very young ones have white gills and we are chary of them. For although we think we know the deadly *Amanita phalloides,* our rule is never to eat a white-gilled mushroom of any kind. Consequently, we are careful to pick only those more mature ones with delicate pink or brown gills.

The mushroom-picking diversion has allowed the tide to catch up with us and we all pile back into the canoe. Even so, the upper flats are still out. The Skiff Hill Channel is plenty deep, but it shoals to nothing when we get up towards our hill. We follow a run which turns and twists through the West Cove flats. For some time it is satisfyingly deep. It peters out, however, just as we are approaching the first bend of the Main Channel. When we come to a stop, there is some talk about getting out and dragging. But the hazards, both psychological and physical, of wading in bare feet through soft mud, are too great. We prefer to wait.

And we are repaid for our waiting. As we sit quietly, an

army of sandpipers lights beside us. Each little bird begins frantically to scurry to and fro, constantly probing the soft surface with his bill, and evidently getting something to his liking. We watch them through our glasses, trying to tell the difference between the semipalmated and the least sandpiper. The least is darker and has greenish legs, and the semipalmated is lighter and has black legs. I am told that each species breeds true. I hope so, as we spend so much time trying to distinguish them.

They look very small beside their cousins with the down-curved bills, the redbacks. The latter, who are winter visitors, seem to specialize on a small, pink worm which they carefully dunk in the water before swallowing.

So engrossed do we become looking for darker backs and greener legs that we are surprised when the canoe suddenly begins to move. The tide is not only rising, it is flooding. We go along with it into the channel, up into the Salt Pond Creek and back to the boathouse. We park the canoe alongside and somewhat wearily trudge up the hill to the Farm House.

But fatigue gives way as we sit on the piazza and sip a refreshing drink. Soon someone will have enough energy to start producing a hearty Farm House meal. Meanwhile, strangely content, we look out over the marsh with its blue water slowly spreading over the flats.

A few of its secrets have this day been bared to us. Sometime, another day will come when conditions are just right. Then perhaps we may wrest more secrets from the Nauset Marsh, as once again we round the Horn.

14. Crickets and Curlew

WHEN you are paddling up the marsh in the foggy, still evening, the sudden, loud chorus of crickets tells you that you are approaching land. Somehow, in the distance, they remind you of sleighbells—if you have ever heard them —as do the "peepers" in spring.

A cricket is a queer insect. Do you know what his long tail is for? He has no neck worth speaking of, and his mouth is not far from the center of that round head of his. Consequently when he finds a succulent morsel on ground or floor, he sticks his tail down and humps up his rear end. Being stiffly made, his head tips down, and the morsel may then be eaten. He is among the few creatures that I know of—the possible exception being the horseshoe crab—that uses his tail instead of his neck.

Crickets come into the Farm House and we love them. When all is quiet, as I have often observed while silently sitting in my chair, they will come out of hiding and make a meal off the gleanings under the dining-room table. It is the greatest good fortune if a cricket climbs up onto a rod case.

That can only mean big doings on tomorrow's expedition. And should a cricket come with us in the canoe, the next day's dinner is assured.

Sometimes we take strange passengers along in the canoe. Just as we pushed off into the creek, not long ago, Char remarked mildly, "I think we have a mouse aboard." As he was then trying to run up under the leg of her dungarees, her extraordinary self-control probably saved us all a wetting. When we got back and had lifted the canoe to its berth beside the boathouse, we flashed a light on. There was the mouse, crowded into the eyes of the boat, as far forward as he could go. His round ears cocked, and his bulging dark eyes riveted on us, he was the picture of resigned courage. We turned over the canoe and went on back up the hill to the house.

The last time I remember having a cricket in the boat was a couple of years ago. We all thought then it was a very good sign. As we reached the mouth of the Beach Channel, the bass began to show, and soon we were in a slather of fish, gulls and terns. If you have never been there, you do not know what excitement is. All around, sometimes within a few feet, bass are tearing at the surface of the water, making a loud sucking noise as they gulp down the bait. The terns scream overhead in a cloud, diving and dipping in graceful curves, while the dark herring gulls, making a peculiarly penetrating squeal, flop around close to the surface and squat down practically on the basses' backs. Harried laughing gulls, especially the young ones (sometimes called "molly gulls"), are squealing too, and ever making a futile dip just too late. Why the old white herring gulls refuse to enter the sport remains a mystery. They seem to think it all beneath their dignity.

Meanwhile, as you paddle around the school of fish, or sometimes, perforce, through it, with two rods out, a double strike seems imminent. And sure enough, both reels begin to sing at once. Now, to keep the lines from crossing requires the utmost skill in handling canoe and rods. Usually one fish breaks off. But we have several times, with the help of Providence—or of the cricket in the boat—landed them both.

In midsummer you may hear a slow, low-pitched cricket's song. My young friend, Fred Lund 3rd, asked me one evening what the sound was. I said it was a field cricket.

"Are you sure?" he asked. "I have an idea it is a green bug."

The thought rankled, and one night I went out onto the lawn with a flashlight. I could hear the "field cricket" quite plainly, but it was extremely difficult to locate the origin of the sound. Finally, as I stood under the black oak, in front of our Newton house, I saw him. He was clinging to the under side of an oak leaf; moreover, he was small and green! He had curiously rounded wings, curved at the edges and rounded like a curled lettuce leaf. He had hoisted his legs—his hind legs, I think—over his back and wings and was scraping them rhythmically. This was the sound I had always thought was made by the much larger field cricket. However, when you listen for it, you will find that the field cricket's song ends with a rising inflection: "Chirr-up," or "Cheer-up," he seems to say. The green bug's song is rather low, and all on the same note. This newly found small cousin of the singers in the field I now know is called the "green tree cricket."

On the dunes, that narrow strip of sand and beach grass which miraculously repels the onslaught of surf and tide, keeping the Nauset Marsh intact, there are many very small crickets less than half an inch long. This is especially true on the upper, or northern end of the beach, where, in areas of sparse beach grass, there is much of that low, dark, moss-like "poverty grass" growing close to the ground. This region is frequented by curlew, who seem to be exceedingly fond of these small crickets. (Foxes, too, eat crickets. In summer I have found fox droppings almost entirely composed of cricket shells.) I should not think the curlew's three- or four-inch bill with its sharp downward curve would be es-

pecially adapted to cricket catching. Come to think of it, I cannot imagine for what purpose such a bill is fitted. It might be good for pulling fiddler crabs out of their holes, but I am sure that if ever a curlew were to swallow a fiddler crab whole, he would very soon regret it. However that may be, I am grateful to the crickets for attracting so many of these striking birds.

When I was a boy, early in 1900, the curlew were exceedingly scarce, but they have steadily increased since their complete protection in 1913. I saw a flock of fifty-four, some ten years ago, which constitutes for me an all-time record. They are handsome birds. The brown tones of their feathers are so soft you want to stroke them. They fly with a rapid wing motion, and appear to move only their wing tips— which is, of course, not the fact. Their call is a harsh, repetitive whistle; only once in a long while will you hear the sweet "curlew" note from which they derive their name. To hear this, you must travel to their breeding grounds far to the north.

Our curlew is the common Hudsonian or jack curlew. Some day I hope to see his very long-billed cousin, the sicklebill; so far, neither he nor I have crossed the continent that we might meet. The smaller, short-billed Eskimo curlew or doughbird, is almost surely extinct, sacrificed to please a gourmet's palate. Will our jack curlew some day reminisce about those delicious Nauset crickets, now extinct because they pleased the curlew palate?

We used to take the children bass fishing on Orleans Beach. We would usually start in time to be there with our rods set up an hour or so before sunset. Taking turn and turn about, we would cast into the sea until darkness had fallen. The waiting fishermen would light a fire to keep themselves warm, and the red sparks snapped up toward the night sky, where stars began to appear like tiny greenish pinpricks, one by one. Finally, wet and tired, we would pack into the car and start back to the Farm House. And all the way, through meadow, swamp, and thicket, the evening would be loud with crickets singing.

Now, years afterward, we think sometimes of sea and beach, bare as it used to be, and of the vast night sky. And in our ears the cricket chorus sounds again as we drive home.

15. *Wind and Weather*

MY ELDEST son, Wyman Jr., considers me a very good long-range weather prophet—"long" taken to mean a prophecy covering the next day's weather. Whenever I make such a forecast, he makes plans for exactly the opposite conditions, and claims to find me very reliable in this respect.

Be that as it may, in our doings at the Farm House we do not need to know the next day's weather. We may lie awake planning what we will do on our forecasted weather, but should it turn out differently, our plans can easily be shifted. It is, however, very important, when we plan our expeditions, to know what the weather is going to do in the next four to six hours. At this I claim to be an expert, in Eastham, anyway.

Here on the Nauset Marsh, our short-range forecasts depend on a knowledge of local weather habits, observation of wind and cloud changes—the "trend," as we call it—and the set to a small barometer in the corner of the living room which, though it records about eight tenths of an inch too high, rises and falls as does any other barometer, sometimes with great celerity.

In winter it is fairly easy. The weather tends to go in cycles. With a high glass, the day will dawn clear. There is either a flat calm, or there are light and variable airs. Visibility is good. Objects stand out in sharp profile. Even the wires on the poles on the East Orleans headland can be seen with the naked eye. Sounds seem to be magnified. Hermie Dill's banging on a tire rim comes sharply across the bay below the hill, and the whistle of the up-freight sounds complainingly clear, even from South Wellfleet. As the surf begins to make up, its ceaseless roar seems to come from close aboard the house.

Shortly the sun's brilliance becomes slightly dulled. An almost invisible "smur" thickens; a light air comes in from the east, and the barometer starts to drop. Such a day, known as a "weather-breeder" on Cape Cod, means a real easterly is in the offing.

While in bed, I can tell by the sound which direction the wind is blowing from—that is, if it has any force. An easterly or northeasterly makes only a loud rushing noise. There is very little banging of this and that, and the windows do not rattle. A nor'wester roars steadily through the cedar at the southwest corner of the house. It roars hard and it roars loud, but it has a clean sound, and when I try to take a sip of water from the glass by my bed, I bump my nose on a skim of ice. A summer sou'wester—that horrid hot blast—rattles and shakes, bangs and batters, blows through the windows and screens, covers sheets and table with dirt, and makes life miserable. This is the "smoky sou'wester," the thinnest wind there is. A good, solid southeaster, on the other hand, smacks the windows with pelting rain, while their loud rattling interferes with sleep. A southeaster drives water through all the windows, but especially the upstairs south window, and loosens the plaster on the living room ceiling.

Let me tell you of a December nor'wester.

The previous day's northeast gale, splashing rain and slush into our faces, drove the tide way over the marsh and flooded our cover just as the ducks started to fly. We came home wet, cold, tired, and discouraged, with very little to show for our efforts. But during the night, the wind backed into the northwest. From time to time, between our dreams, the steady roar from the cedars proclaimed its presence, as did also the cold toes and the cold nose.

The alarms, two of them just for safety, start their clatter at four-fifteen. The wise one, who has slept in his woolly underwear, builds a quick fire in the fireplace, before which he bundles up for the coming ordeal. A quick breakfast of coffee, bacon, and eggs is prepared on the oil stove. The coal stove is also started, to keep the pump from freezing. Come to think of it, better trip the pump anyway; the thermometer outside the kitchen window records eighteen degrees.

Then comes the stumbling walk down the hill, burdened with gun, shells, water (which will freeze), and lunch (which will also freeze). The wind blows stark from the northwest, so strong that to look into it numbs the face and makes the eyes water. Anticipatory excitement is tempered by a real feeling of fear. Can we make it, and get back safely?

Already a red dawn begins to show, and fast-scurrying, purple clouds become salmon-tinted. Quickly we stow away our gear and push off into the dark water.

It is a simple trip down the marsh—that is, if the tide is either up or down. But beware the half tide. Under such conditions, it takes long experience, real knowledge, and a considerable amount of luck to find your way out to the Main Channel through the winding run from the Salt Pond Creek. Otherwise, it's a fair wind, and only your left arm gets tired trying to keep your gunning float from yawing.

Likely it's Byzoon Cove you are headed for, a spot little appreciated by the rank and file. Incidentally, a "byzoon" is the ideal duck day: the wind from the nor'west, at thirty-two miles per hour; the temperature 28.5 degrees Fahrenheit, and four-minute snow squalls every twenty minutes. Many neophytes make the mistake of calling all-out gales or storms, especially those from the northwest, byzoons. This is greatly to be deplored, as such storms lead to much suffering and usually to little game.

Byzoon Cove is the place to be, in a typical byzoon. It is one of the few places on the Nauset Marsh where one can shoot black ducks on a lee shore. This is much to be desired, as otherwise, if there is a fly of birds, many shots will be lost when you are in the boat to retrieve your game.

Daylight comes. Your shooting is highly inaccurate. Why shouldn't it be, you say, when you are facing into a gale of wind, when you are bundled up to the ears, and when your fingers even inside your mittens are so numb you cannot tell thumb from forefinger? Still and all, you have accumulated several days' supply of dinner. Many ducks have come sliding in on stiff wings. When really close, the light streak about the face looks almost white. How could you miss such an easy shot? Did you allow for windage?

Comes lunch time. The cold chicken is really cold, so cold it has to be thawed in the mouth before it can be eaten. The water bottle is half frozen, but not broken. Fortunately, one does not need much water under such conditions. The thermos bottle of once hot coffee is almost more than cold hands can deal with and turns out only a lukewarm brew.

Meanwhile, ice is forming all the time. The decoys' heads get so iced that they capsize. Slur begins to change to cake ice. You wonder about the upper channels. Are they getting plugged? The day wanes; as the sun drops, the cold increases. And all of a sudden, the thought of the cozy Farm House becomes irresistible.

Then starts the long fight home against the ebb. You watch a clamshell on the bottom, where the tide runs strong by Pull Devil Corner. You see it first just forward of the forward oar post. You pull and pull, and then you see it amidships. Pull, pull some more, and finally it disappears astern. After a long, long while you get under the lee of the hill and coast back to the boathouse.

Finally the last, long, weary trudge up the hill, the "clumpf" of boots on the platform, the breaking of guns to make sure that they are unloaded, and, as the door is opened, that indescribable, delicious Farm House smell. The house seems warm at first. But no sooner are outer layers peeled than it becomes apparent that it is not warm. There is ice in the water pitcher. Before long, however, fires are roaring and warming drinks forthcoming. It wasn't so bad, after all, down there on the marsh.

I make no apologies for shooting ducks, and no excuses.

Nature, in many respects, seems very cruel. I remember watching a garter snake trying to swallow a wood frog. The snake had the frog by one leg, and the frog was trying to hop away by means of the other. My sympathies were with the frog, but I did not interfere. It seemed to me that the snake had as much right on his side as did the frog on his. (As it happened, the frog won out.) Man is an omnivorous animal, and, to satisfy his carnivorous needs, destroys countless other animals. I get a primitive satisfaction in hunting and fishing—supplying food by my own efforts.

So it is that Farm House Rule 1 reads that anything shot must be eaten. (A later amendment excepted rats, mice and fur-bearing animals.) Consequently, especially when a boy, I came to eat many strange things, including hawk, gull, grebe, night heron, and crow. If properly prepared, they are all good, except crow.

A nor'wester is a fighting man's wind. It blows clean and strong. It knows the rules and plays the game. It may lick you in a fair fight, but at least you know what you are dealing with.

Not so one of those cussed sou'westers. It's the sneakiest wind there is. Suppose you are out sailing a light boat. With some pride, by leaning way out to windward, you go through the strongest puff with full sail, only to capsize to windward as the breeze suddenly quits.

It's a fussy wind, a complaining wind. It shrieks through the screens one minute, and heaves a subsiding sigh the next. It's a humid wind. It cakes the salt shakers, and mildews the sails. It's a lasting wind. It's a horrid wind.

For days on end, sometimes for nearly two weeks, the

canoe will stay land-bound. Each day, more and more scud clouds make up, the haze thickens, and you think a good rain will clear things up. But not so. This is just one of the sou'wester's tricks. It makes you think it is bringing on a good rain that will freshen the crops and fill the well, but just as it becomes darkest, a sudden ray of sunshine streaks across the southern sky, and the next moment it is hazy and hot again.

About all a sou'wester is good for, here at the Farm House, is fishing off the beach. One must admit that a good fresh southwest breeze will carry an eel a long way out to sea—not that it matters much, but it does make you feel that your fishing has somehow become more important, if not more dignified. Trouble is, these sou'westers frequently blow so hard that they blow the sand. Have you ever been on the Nauset Beach when the sand was blowing? Well, you don't want to be.

We go fishing with bare feet and bare legs, and the sand stings us like a thousand biting ants. We perforce take to the water, where we become thoroughly soaked by underestimating the "swooshers." There may be an easterly swell, even in a southwester. You learn to figure the big seas. They pile up higher and higher, pound down, not far from your feet, and sweep up the rise with a regularity that is easily dealt with. But beware the swoosher. It does not look like much. It is not a high wave, and frequently follows docilely the path of its bigger brother. But it carries a lot of power. Without noise or fuss it comes welling up the rise and, catching you completely off guard, soaks you from fore to aft, mostly aft.

If you figured on supper on the beach and dumped a basket of food, extra clothing, and extra reel there, better leave it. Neither food, nor clothing, nor reel will ever be any good again. Unless you have a gizzard, you cannot use the food, your great-grandchildren will still find sand in their inherited clothing, and the reel will squeak and grind forever after.

Smoky sou'westers are most frequent in July and August. If you plan on coming down to the Farm House, better wait until September. Even then, you may not escape.

October is a wonderful month at Eastham. Summers are cool, for here the Cape is only four miles wide and most breezes (except the sou'wester) come across the water. But when night temperatures consistently go well below the water temperatures—as they do in late September and after—we have warmer weather than further inland, where the land at night cools sharply. The Cape has, therefore, a late fall.

One day in October, my son Fred and I decided to see if we could get some meat for dinner, the quota for the crew being two black ducks. We left the house in the very early dawn, with the temperature at thirty-six degrees. There was not a breath of air. The hollows were filled with "river damp," and, to the east, looked like tiny lakes. As we descended the hill, it got noticeably colder and the steel of our gun barrels became too cold for the bare hand.

When we pushed out of the Salt Pond Creek, the stars were shining brightly, and we could just make out the cupola of the Town Hall to the west. Three minutes later, we rowed into what seemed like a dense fog, yet the stars still shone brightly, and the top of our hill was clearly visible. It was a curious sensation. We could not make out any of the landmarks, or perhaps better, "marsh" marks. We could neither

find First Hummock nor Uncle Heeman's Creek. Yet all
the while the upper shore line was visible.

By compass bearing we got to the easterly 'Tween Channels Hummock, where we made a good set. But as the sun
rose (according to our watches), the river damp thickened
until we became immersed in a really dense fog—dense overhead, that is, as well as below. We wondered why this was,
and concluded that the rising sun was causing an upward
movement of the mist. Unidentified fowl would suddenly
loom over our decoys, and as suddenly disappear. Sometimes
we fired a futile shot; sometimes we were too late even for
that. A gull or two would silently glide overhead in ghostly
dimness.

Not until nearly an hour and a half after sunrise did the
sun's warmth absorb the fog. Suddenly all was clear. It was
not like a sea fog rolling away or gradually lifting; one moment we were in complete isolation, with a two hundred-
foot limit of visibility, and the next moment we could see a
ship, hull down, six or seven miles out to sea.

By hook or by crook, we did get our two ducks in spite of
the flat calm—a calm so complete that Fred blew a smoke
ring clear across the channel. At ten o'clock we gave up and
lazed back up the channel, the now hot rays of the sun making us devoutly wish we had forgotten about heavy woollies.
On our way back over the flats, we picked up a half basket of
scallops which had suddenly appeared in the bay below our
hill, and proudly we struggled up to the house, with a royal
meal in the making.

Unless it be a question of beach fishing, a "dry northeaster" is one of our best winds. Come with us to the Cape

in late March or early April and you will likely run into one.

This is a wonderful time of year to stay at the Farm House. There are no activities possible which require a huge amount of thought and effort, such as duck shooting or bass fishing. The only fishing at this time is flounder fishing. Though the flounders may run large (my wife caught one of four-and-one-fourth pounds), it is ordinarily very cold sport, and the fun is tempered by the thought of filleting.

There comes a morning in late March when the brightness of the rising sun, shining through the south window, wakes you at six-thirty. The floor is cold; the house is cold. You build a quick fire in the fireplace, having remembered to get the logs and kindling ready the night before. Your first weather observation comes only after you have fully, but not too warmly, dressed before the fire. The thermometer reads thirty-eight degrees, the wind is fresh from the northeast, the sky is clear, and the air is full of the finest champagne.

The thing to do on such a day is to walk down the beach to the Inlet and back. At ten o'clock you start off, full of energy, blowing all the dust-laden, worry-burdened city air out of your system, and replacing it with the clean, fresh, salt-tangy breeze from the sea.

First you skirt the Cedar Bank. So high it is, that you can see the whole marsh laid out before you. You will find six Canada geese on the Minister's Flat, the old gander standing erect, neck outstretched, only occasionally taking time out to find some succulent root. You will find black ducks, mostly in pairs, darker blobs on the dark sedge which has been cropped short by the winter's ice. You will see whistlers (goldeneyes) fly up the channel, stop, turn, and light with unbelievable suddenness, and, if the wind is not too strong, you may hear the musical winnowing of the cock whistler's wings.

Further along, by Clam Diggers Headquarters, you will find a flock of about twenty-five buffleheads, those tiny fast-flying ducks, the male with a pie-shaped piece of white transecting his lovely iridescent purple head. In the pines by Little Creek you will start out eight or ten hardy night herons which have spent the winter there, unless that fierce marauder, the great horned owl, has cleaned them out. By the marsh shore, you skirt the cliff, atop which is perched the Nauset Coast Guard Station, and start your walk down the beach.

It is best to go down the beach on the inside—that is, on the marsh side—just why, I do not know. You may see various kinds of fowl on the way down, and surely many black ducks. Horned larks will fly past in loose flocks, uttering their curious thin little note. ("Pippy birds," we used to call them.) If you are lucky, you will see, on the top of a Coast Guard telephone pole, a snowy owl. As you approach fairly close, his neckless head appears to turn around and around, while his baleful brassy eye glares menacingly at you.

When you get to the Inlet Run, a deep pool that comes up to a sandy beach will tempt you, and you may take a swim —or more accurately, a dip—and dry off in the lee of a high dune, where the wind has undercut a "hen bank."

Finally you reach the Inlet, where a fast ebb is boiling out through a deep channel. Further out, where the channel shoals, the current meets the surge of oncoming seas carried by the force of the fresh northeast breeze. From bar to bar, across the mouth, all is a smother of white, and only the experienced eye can tell where the channel runs. Better not count on the Nauset Marsh for a safe landfall. Only hardy lobstermen in powerful motorboats regularly go in and out, and very few of them.

Then comes the turn back on the outer beach, the Great Beach, that stretches from the tip of Monomoy to Race Point at Provincetown. As you gaze north and south, the beach gives you a feeling of infinity; it seems as if it must go on and on as it disappears into the haze of breaking surf. Not so the horizon, sharp and clear, broken only by the lumpiness of the sea. It seems shaped like the edge of a saucer, and appears to curve comfortingly back to land.

The sting of the breeze off the sea gives you fresh energy, as first you try walking the soft sand at the top of the rise, and then the wet sand at the bottom, where you have to be

nimble to avoid a wetting. Stunning white gannets, their black wing tips hardly visible, glide to windward over wave crest and into trough with almost no effort. A curious seal pops his dog-like head out of the water at forty yards and, reappearing every hundred yards or so, follows you along all the way to the Coast Guard Station. And if you are lucky, you will hear a sweet, soft whistle, and if you look sharp, you will see a light-colored stone suddenly start to run on twinkling feet. It's a piping plover, whose cheery note and beady black eye tender you a wary welcome.

It is a long walk up the beach, but the invigorating air has sustained you. Now comes the hard part. You have left the beach at the Coast Guard cut-through, and again have reached the pines at Little Creek, where the night herons were, known to us as the "Quawkery." Better stop for ten minutes' rest and look over the marsh with the glasses. You *might* see a European widgeon, and you will very likely see eight or ten of the big pond sheldrake, or goosanders, for they seem to like the region of Little Creek.

It is hard to heave your bulk off the mossy sand at the Quawkery and start the last lap back. No skirting the Cedar Bank now. It is a straight course to the Farm House. You pass the shallow pond and for the twenty-first time put the glasses on the dark object on the further shore, and discover it to be a stump. Then down by the pond-hole back of the barn, where once we saw a pair of wood ducks, and once a single scaup, and often a black duck or two. And so up the last long hill to the weather-beaten Farm House, which looks as if it had been standing there for centuries.

For a moment, we stand on the platform and look south off across the marsh. The low hills in front of us are a warm brown. Through the dip between our hill and the Cedar Bank we see the marsh whose wide channels and bays are today almost a robin's-egg blue, contrasting with the dark brown of the winter sedge. Further out is the thin line of dunes along which we have just walked, the wind-swept hollows, white where the sun strikes, dark in shadow, both encircled by the yellow-green of the surrounding beach grass. And still further out, except where hidden by the highest dunes, stretches a gentian-blue ocean which seems to sparkle and dance.

Our legs are weary and we tumble gratefully into our chairs. It is not such a long walk, perhaps seven or eight miles. But a mile on that beach is a very long mile indeed. Right now, unless something about dinner needs doing, we are content to sit in our chairs, or perhaps on the edge of the platform, and watch the marsh and the sea; watch that marsh hawk as he hangs on an updraft over the hill, motionless, as if suspended by an invisible wire, and casts a sharp eye for motion in the grass below; watch the gulls, soaring higher and higher, apparently just for the fun of it, for frequently they come back to the point from which they started; watch a white cloud as it drifts across a clear blue sky; or just watch.

Yes, come down to the Farm House in late March or early April, and hope for a dry northeaster. It will blow all the musty cobwebs from your mind, clear your lungs, and put a zip into your blood which will carry you through many a weary day.

We were at the Farm House on September 21st, 1938, the day of the "first hurricane." We left the house about half past four in the afternoon on a mushroom hunt. The wind was then blowing out of the southeast, and freshening. It is a Farm House rule that a breeze which hangs to the southeast and freshens in the late afternoon, or after sunset, bodes ill.

We found few mushrooms, and, besides, the breeze became so strong that it blew the ones we had found out of the colanders we had taken along to put them in. So we eased home from the Cedar Bank before the wind. The old folks stopped at the house, but Marg and Char, then ten and thirteen years old and delighted with the feel of it, went romping off to leeward. Suddenly I began to have some qualms.

"If you can't get back, stop at the Riches'!" we called out.

By now it was blowing really pert, still straight from the southeast, and dark clouds were getting heavier as they raced past overhead. We went down to the boathouse, my wife and I, to see if all was snug. I remember thinking, as I peeked around the corner of the boathouse, that I would hate to be out shooting in such a wind, and wondered if two of us could row against it. I noted two winter yellowlegs, unable to make straight to windward, taking long tacks, finally giving up and lighting on the edge of the Salt Pond Creek.

When we got back to the house, we were relieved to find the children safely ensconced. I went out to shut the barn door, for I thought the wind might shift to the southwest, and blow nearly directly into the barn. Somehow, with the door open, it seemed too much like a huge spinnaker set in a gale of wind. The barn might take off for the Coast Guard Station. I got the door shut all right and stepped out from the corner. The next thing I knew, I was flat on my face. Then I realized we were up against something unusual. I admit a weight of two-hundred-and-twenty pounds, and I do not easily blow over.

In the house there was a continuous roar of sound, and heavy spats of rain slammed at the windows. At six o'clock there was a sudden and complete lull, with blue sky above. You, as well as the house, seemed to feel it necessary to brace against the wind, and the tendency was to fall over to windward. Twenty minutes later, the clouds shut down, and the wind slatted into the southwest, hauling later to the west-southwest. It blew harder, if anything, and started the frames of one of the south doors and of the south bedroom window. I had to spike them down.

But we were snug and didn't really think much of it. I

thought I was bold when I recorded in the log an estimated wind velocity of seventy-five miles per hour at the peak. We went to bed happy and serene, with no worries.

The next day, we still did not think much about it. To be sure, they came over from the new house, which is dependent on electricity for its modern gadgets, to get some pump water. Later, they came with perishable food to put in our ice box, and rather diffidently asked if they might use our privy. We were, of course, delighted to accommodate, and sent them back with a couple of our kerosene lamps. It was not until the following day that we realized the impact of the storm.

All this came to me the other day when Tom, who delivers ice for us, seemed much puzzled.

"I can't understand these hurricanes," says he. "Here one hit Florida, and then turned right 'round and hit it again. Sometimes, when I try to think too much, I get be-wildered." And then, after a long pause, "Sometimes I think it's better not to think too much."

I agree.

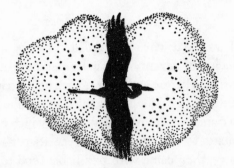

16. Fog

FOG! The terror of all navigators, whether on land, on sea, or in the air. Great is its power, for it can slow down and stop all moving wheels, spoil the lawn party at the Casino, cut into the resort proprietor's net, and incite the Browns to wrangling again due to their all-night foghorn sleeplessness. I well remember my Prides Crossing friend's annoyance when I told him that his snoring had kept me awake all night.

"That was the Baker's Island foghorn," he explained.

What is fog? The answer is easy. Fog is a cloud. Whenever you are in a cloud, you are in fog. If you are either above or below fog, it becomes a cloud. What is a cloud? A cloud is a mass of water vapor which has condensed into fine particles of water. What is rain? Never mind.

Why is fog? Generalities are easy. "Fog occurs when warm, moisture-laden air meets cold air." Therefore, heavy fog belts are found where warm and cold ocean currents meet. Also fog occurs when there is a considerable difference between a suddenly lowered air temperature and the temperature of large bodies of water, such as, for instance, the river damp which hangs over pond and river during the night and early dawn of a still, cold May or October morning, or the "steam" that rises from the ocean on a below-zero day, and causes such havoc with shipping traffic. But why fog suddenly appears in a certain area, and as suddenly vanishes in the same area, I have never understood.

The waters of outer Cape Cod are in the "heavy fog belt," which I believe means that fog occurs, on the average, on one out of every three days. Fortunately for us at the Farm House, the fog frequently hangs offshore, where it can sometimes be seen as a low-lying, rather ominous wall of cloud. Perhaps it will drift in and off the lower end of the Nauset Marsh, blotting out for a time the East Orleans headland; occasionally, it will shut down thick across the entire Cape and smother us in a blanket of moisture.

The next day, likely as not, a hot, muggy sou'wester will blow endless strands of fog across and away to the east, the sun gradually lifting them higher and higher into "fog clouds" until finally the sky is clear. Be sure you have your compass, though, for when the sun drops, the wind may drop too. Then that sudden chill east air strikes your cheek, and you find yourself alone in a strange world, landmarks obliterated, familiar objects distorted. Birds do not like fog; neither do I.

Once when I was a boy, Mel Marble, our skipper, took me out in my father's twenty-one-foot catboat, the "Kingfisher," to Cleveland's Ledge in order to bottom fish. Cleveland's Ledge, incidentally, was discovered by my father and

Mel Marble when they were trolling for bluefish in the middle of Buzzards Bay with a two-pound lead tied one-hundred-and-fifty feet out on a three-hundred-foot line. The wind unexpectedly petered out, and the lead caught in a rocky ledge. A quick jibe saved line and lead, and soon a little sounding demonstrated a large group of rocks. I believe they anchored at once and caught a good mess of rock (sea) bass and tautog. President Cleveland, who spent his summers at Gray Gables at the head of the bay, and who was a great fisherman, was told of this spot and came so often to fish it that it has been known ever since as "Cleveland's Ledge."

On the present occasion, a heavy fog shut in, and with it came a light northeast air. Does the east wind bring the fog, or the fog bring the east wind?

Anyway, we fished for a spell and then decided to make our way in. Mel got out the box compass, and we headed by dead reckoning for Marion Harbor. The jaws of the gaff creaked loudly as the uneasy swell swung the sail inboard and then slatted it back. But through it all came the clear, steady tones of the Bird Island fog bell.

"Gee, this is easy," I said.

Mel said: "Humph!"

We kept the bell to starboard as we slowly made our close-hauled way. The bell suddenly sounded very loud.

"We're going ashore on Southeast Ledge, Mel," I said, in some perturbation.

Mel smiled, said nothing, and kept his eye on the compass. Then, just as suddenly, the sound of the bell stopped. I waited a while, and then I got scared.

"Why did they stop it?" I asked Mel.

"Didn't," said he. "Noises hop around in a fog."

Just then the red Centreboard Ledge buoy loomed out. Our craft did not draw very much water, and we left the buoy a hundred yards to port, at which point we were dead to leeward of Bird Island and very close to it. No fog bell. Later on, when we came upon the black Seal Rocks buoy, and left it, also, carefully to port, the bell suddenly became insistently loud. Since then I have often observed that sounds, in a light air, can best be heard across the wind. At the Farm House we hear the whistling buoy, or "grunter," off the Inlet, which is southeast of us, in a southwest air, and sometimes, when the breeze is southeast, we hear the whistler off the Peaked Hill Bar to the northeast.

Fog can do queer things. In 1914 I was traveling east on a Cunard liner, three days out of Boston, bound for Liverpool. I woke about a half-hour after sunrise and looked out through my porthole to the north. I was quite stunned. No one had told me that our course took us so close to Sable Island. I knew that the southern end of it bore only a hair north of east from Boston Harbor, but I certainly felt sure that our three days out of port meant we were in mid-ocean. I looked again to make certain. I could see a small white church, with pointed spire and a round shadow that suggested a clock. The land rose sharply from the sea, and a cluster of houses was grouped about the entrance to what I supposed was a snug harbor. Above sea level, large patches of evergreens, presumably spruces, bordered lighter pastures where I thought I could make out herds of cattle.

I was amazed, and for fully five minutes kept my eyes glued to the porthole. Then things seemed to change. The church disappeared, and so did the houses. Precipitous mountains and dark valleys took their place. And then the whole island suddenly became the edge of a fog bank, the quartering, rising sun having cast all sorts of peculiar shadows. Ever since that moment I have been skeptical of the old saying: "Seeing is believing."

Fog can do other queer things. Some years ago, a friend and I sat in the grass on Porchy Marsh, at the spot where the then high, sandy Porchy Bar made out across the channel toward Teal Hummock. It was a sultry September afternoon, and soon the fog shut in thick. Shooting in thick fog is not much fun, for the fun of shooting lies in being out-of-doors, in a pleasant spot, with a good view both of the surrounding landscape and of the passing wildlife. In a fog, one's world is limited to a three-hundred-foot radius. Nothing is seen except for an unexpected, ghostlike apparition which turns out to be a herring gull. Occasionally, the clear, peewee-like notes of a black-breasted plover, or the more staccato call of the yellowlegs, bring forth from us a burst of frantic, and usually ineffective, whistled imitations. A flock or two of peep will suddenly swirl over our heads, so close as nearly to remove our hats.

On this occasion, just before dark, we had a shot at a bunch of summer (lesser) yellowlegs, and, after a vast amount of banging, we managed to bag one—small pickings for two hungry men. As darkness suddenly began to fall, we picked up and started to row across the channel toward the just visible Middle Flat. Halfway across, we wondered if we had remembered to put our game inside the boat. We both rummaged around in the cockpit, finally found the bird, and looked up. We could still make out both the Porchy and the Middle Flat shore. We continued on our way home. Fifteen minutes later, when we should have been off Uncle Heeman's Creek, I became uneasy. We came to a wide creek, but even in spite of the tide, it looked too big and did not run off at the correct angle. I took out my compass. We were headed *south*, out near the Inlet, instead of north, just off the Cedar Bank and nearly home.

It gave me a shock I have never forgotten. Of course, what had happened was that when we were both busy looking for our bird, the boat had made a one-hundred-and-eighty-degree turn. When we looked up, the relative positions of the dimly seen shore lines remained the same, and we went south instead of north. I was glad I had taken my compass with me; indeed, without it, we might have become involved in some real difficulty. Since then, I have never gone out, either in the Nauset Marsh, or on the West Shore flats, or in the woods, without a compass.

In *"Roccus Lineatus,"* I have told of the spooks a foggy night on the beach can produce. Even a foggy day on the beach, especially if one is alone, may give one the creeps, although perhaps not to the extent of bringing about a precipitate retreat. My brother was casting off the beach into the fog one afternoon, and working north along the shore. He came to a man sitting at the top of the rising behind him.

"Any luck?" asked Harry, backing up the beach as he reeled in.

There was no answer. Harry turned around and saw to his chagrin that he was addressing a lobster pot which had washed ashore.

I had somewhat the same experience. I had the feeling someone was watching me cast, and, as usual under such circumstances, got myself a bad backlash. Hastily, I backed up the beach and bumped into what I took to be my audience.

"Excuse me," I said politely, and turned to face an empty orange crate.

My daughter, Margie, and I took the canoe out early one black morning. As we left the boathouse at the Salt Pond Creek, a perceptible lightening of the previously black darkness suggested that possibly the almanac was right. We crept along under the Cedar Bank, which by now could easily be made out, and fished up the Cedar Bank Channel. Gradually, the light increased, but we could not see much afield. After quite a long while, the cupola of the Nauset Coast Guard Station suddenly appeared and we found ourselves close to the bluff at the head of Nauset Bay. There was no evidence of bird or any other life. However, as we turned back and headed into the Minister's Channel, our friend, the musical crow, could be heard calling from the vicinity of the Cedar Bank.

A short distance below Minister's Point, which marks the junction of the Minister's Channel with the Beach Run to form the Beach Channel, Marg hooked into a fish, and, after a few minutes, brought a nice two-pound bass to the net. This area, between White's shanty and the cut-through below White's, has not infrequently produced a fish. (One of my friends, however, complains that these directions are insufficient, inasmuch as White's house, some ten years ago, was completely washed away during an exceptional tide and storm, and the cut-through has for at least five years been blocked by rapidly growing sand dunes.) When at last we paddled out by Caleb's Hummock at the mouth of the Beach Channel, quite happy to have caught a fish, the general brightness indicated that the sun was up. However, ex-

cept for Caleb's Hummock and the opposite nearby edge of the Middle Flat, we could see nothing. Our world became a peculiarly spherical one, limited to a narrow two-hundred-foot radius. I took my compass out and put it on the canoe bottom before me. For, below the mouth of the Beach Channel, there is a stretch of wide water at high tide.

"Look," I said, pointing. "There is a man fishing on the Porchy riffles."

I could see him standing up in a skiff and casting.

"Yes," said Marg. "We'd better not go too near him."

"I hear he has caught a lot of fish that way," I remarked, as I headed away to give him plenty of room.

Just then he rose from the water and flew off. He had suddenly turned into a young, dark herring gull.

On another occasion, during the war, my daughter Char and I made almost the same circuit in the midst of a thick fog. On our way home, we heard the loud roaring of motors.

"Lost airplane," I said and shuddered a bit. "Thick fog, no radio direction, gas low, hoping for a safe crash landing."

We paddled harder, the engines roared louder, and soon we saw the huge hull of a flying boat coming to rest off the First Hummock, across the channel from the Cedar Bank. We really made time, pushing the canoe so fast as to make her dip with every stroke. And then, suddenly, our crippled airplane began more and more to take the shape of a motorboat. When finally we came close, it turned out to be a cabin cruiser trying to get out on the top of an unusually high tide, and well stuck on the flat just across from First Hummock. What in the world, we thought, was a boat of this draught doing inside the Nauset Marsh? We told the disgruntled and somewhat truculent skipper where the channel was (he found it on the evening tide), and ever since have been skeptical as to his occupation.

The suddenness of fog is one of its worst features. Last summer, we went out in the canoe at high water, a couple of hours before sunset. It was a beautiful, warm afternoon, with almost no wind and a clear sky. We again cruised over the Nauset Bay flats, but found no bass. On our way down the Minister's Channel we could see umbrella handles here and there, sticking up out of the marsh grass. Occasionally, one would suddenly straighten out, and a great, ungainly, yet strangely graceful, loose-jointed hulk of a bird would leisurely take off, trailing long legs behind and eventually curling its neck back over its shoulders. The great blue herons like the Middle Flat, and, at high water, in September and October, collect in loose groups, each bird striking a different pose. One will stand erect, sharp beak lifted and gleaming yellow eye turned skyward; another hunches up, halving his size, draws in his neck, cocks his head, and eyes the water beneath him. If, luckily, you have him in the field of your glasses, and if he does not suspect your presence, you may see a sudden motion. So fast is the strike that only the obvious swallowing undulation of the neck, with head uplifted, indicates the destiny of a hapless minnow.

A half hour before sunset finds you out of the Beach Channel below Caleb's Hummock, just as the ebb begins to sweep across the Goose Hummock flats, by every rule the time of times to catch a fish. But the fish do not seem to know the rules and there is no excitement. And then, silently and relentlessly, small puffets of fog come drifting across the dunes "on little cat feet." A slight chill creeps up your spine; the extra sweater is retrieved from under the bow. Old Sol, a moment ago so strong and invincible, suddenly begins to lose his power. A cold air from the east riffles the water. And then, all at once, your world is blotted out. Abruptly, the roar of the surf seems close aboard.

"Let's get back," you say, somewhat casually, as you fish for the compass in the bottom of the tackle bag.

Now, as darkness rapidly descends, the thought of the Farm House seems good. A fire, so out of place this hot noon, is highly desirable. You put a bit more drive to your chunking paddles, follow up the Porchy shore and around Tom Doane's Hummock, and take a bearing just west of northwest from Puli Devil Corner. The gray dimness becomes darker, all landmarks disappear, and you wonder whether the black or the white end of the compass needle points to north. Fortunately, you have scratched the formula on the back of the case: "B=N." Of a sudden, the cricket chorus hits your consciousness. Then a strange headland, with an unusual pattern of cedars, looms out of the fog. Where are you? This is unfamiliar ground. Perhaps you got turned around. This looks like the lower end of Skiff Hill. No! Here is the Salt Pond Creek and there is the boathouse. You are safe in port. Now it seems ridiculous to have been so, yes, scared. The weather is warm, the marsh landlocked except for a narrow inlet; real harm is well-nigh impossible. And yet—and yet, the fog gets you down. You want home. And you are afraid you are not going to get there.

And then, at home at last after the long climb up the hill, standing before a crackling fire with a glass in hand containing just a smitch of bourbon, you forget your fear. Fog is not bad; it is good fishing weather. There is usually little or no wind, and the bright sun, with its dark shadows, is dimmed and does not frighten the fish. You must make an early start tomorrow.

Fog! Terror of all navigators! Yes, even on the Nauset Marsh, you cast your spell and bring a chill to the stoutest heart. Birds do not like you; neither do I.

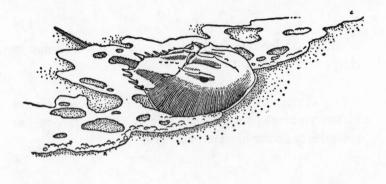

17. *Tide*

"TIME and tide," so it is said, "wait for no man." On the Nauset Marsh, this proverb might be paraphrased: "There is no man who has not waited for the tide." Around the tide center all our activities. What, then, is this mysterious thing we call tide?

Unless one is an expert physicist and well up on calculus, one should not inquire too deeply into this subject. I have no real understanding of the complexities of the tide, and no new ideas about its vagaries. What I have learned has come bit by bit, pieced together from the understandable portions of learned books, and from wise counsel. Here, then, are a few thoughts about tides in general, and especially about the tides of the Nauset Marsh.

There are four kinds of waves: wind waves, storm waves, earthquake waves, and tide waves.

Wind waves are just that—waves caused by the wind. I do not know how much wind it takes to make a riffle over a previously glassy sea; it may depend somewhat on whether the water is clean or slightly greasy. However, I have seen racing rigs, such as the "110," moving through what looked like a flat calm, not only with steerageway, but also with a bow wave. Possibly the high Marconi type of sail catches upper air currents not apparent at sea level. In any case it is certain that as the wind increases the waves get higher. According to Lecky (*Wrinkles in Practical Navigation*), the height of a wave in a real gale can be determined by the formula: 1.5 times the square root of the "fetch." The latter may be considered to be the distance to the windward shore. On our outer beach, the fetch is the coast of Spain, which is considerably over two thousand five hundred miles away. According to this ratio, the height of the waves in a wind of gale force should be 1.5×50—or seventy-five feet. Fortunately, we do not have such waves; no wind wave reaches such height, though an earthquake wave may. The answer to this riddle, of course, must be that the fetch can apply only to the area involved by a wind of constant direction. This distance is not likely to be over one hundred fifty miles, assuming this to be the radius of a storm system. This brings our equation down to 1.5×12—or eighteen feet—still a good-sized wave.

Wind waves pound the shores—big ones outside, small ones inside our marsh. Without them, life would be tame indeed. We welcome them when we are shooting, damn them when fishing. And we stand, awed and humbled, on the great beach, as wave after wave comes rolling in from the east, rearing skyward ever higher, cresting and spilling white on the outer bar, then tripping on the edge of the shelf, curling, and crashing into foam at our feet. They do little material damage when the water is low. The dunes are undercut and houses washed away when the tide is high.

Storm waves are not wind waves, though of course the latter will be increased in storms. A storm wave may occur when there is a sharp gradient between the central low barometric pressure and an outside high. Consequently, water tends to hump up under the low area, and this constitutes the storm wave. It may occur as a single wave, or as a series of waves. When the low-pressure area passes at the time of high water, the storm wave is added to the tide wave, and a very high tide may result.

In the hurricane of 1938, we were told that there was a pressure difference of two inches, representing a drop of the barometer from a high of 30.5 to a low of 28.5 inches. Such a drop would mean a difference in actual pressure of one pound per square inch, again distributed over a radius of less than one hundred fifty miles. At about 6:00 P.M., near the high of a big "spring" tide, the center of the storm passed over Buzzards Bay. In addition the wind had a southerly slant, and further tended to pile water into the bay. The result was the most extreme tide ever recorded, and the damage to property was unbelievable. As the low passed, the storm wave receded, and caused powerful ebb-tide currents that carried many people to their deaths.

Late one summer, when I was about ten years old, we were struck by a very severe storm at Marion, on Buzzards Bay. It was not a hurricane, but it certainly could have been classed as a full gale, with winds over sixty miles per hour. The wind came from the southeast. High water was due at noon, but by 9:00 A.M. the tide had already reached the level of a normal spring tide, and my father began to get really worried. At this moment, the wind snapped around to the northwest, and soon was blowing just as hard as before. Shortly thereafter, the tide started to ebb, and, in an hour and a half, went lower than any of us had ever seen it. So strong was the tide that channel spars were dragged completely under water. Then back again it came, so that at high water at noon, a level was reached almost as great as a normal neap tide. The following ebb was normal and orderly.

Naturally, I was curious about this amazing phenomenon. Someone told me the wind-shift had "blown the water out." I never quite accepted this theory, but it was many years before I discovered the probable explanation. The storm must have been a small "tight" system, with a sharp pressure gradient, causing a definite storm wave. As is common with all types of waves, instead of appearing as a single wave it came as a series of waves, much as a stone thrown into a pond produces not one, but a series of waves. When the low pressure area passed, the trough of the main wave caused an ebb that went through the normal flood; the next ripple came along with the normal flood. Undoubtedly, there followed minor oscillations which were not observed.

In severe storm systems, then, a low pressure, or "partial vacuum," may cause a "lifting" of the water sufficient to produce a high water at the shore. When this coincides with normal high water, great damage may result.

Earthquake waves are due to great upheavals of the ocean floor, and have more commonly occurred in the Pacific area. They are sometimes associated with the appearance of new volcanic islands. As a result of such upheavals, huge waves may roll along the ocean surface for many miles. When they reach the shore, they trip themselves up like any other waves, thunder up beaches, and, if confined to a gradually narrowing estuary, may actually form a wall of water many feet high. Such waves may cause untold property damage and great loss of life, the latter especially, because these waves are frequently unexpected and unpredicted. Large steamers may be left high and dry on the shore, and all shore installations ruined.

The last earthquake wave that I know of occurred not long ago in Hawaii, and there are many people now in this country who can give eyewitness accounts of it.

Tide waves are caused by the pull of the moon's, and—to a lesser extent because of its distance—the sun's, gravity; and they are the cause of what we call tide. It would be wise to stop right here; but let's try to go a little farther.

If the world were covered with water (and especially if it were eighteen miles deep, for some obscure reason), and if then the sun were directly opposite to the moon—at the "full moon," in other words—the water would hump up under the sun and under the moon, and as a consequence be depressed in the regions in between. Furthermore, if the sun and moon should be close together, or at the "new moon," the same thing would happen. Do not ask why. It seems the earth does not like having a big hump of water on one side, without having a big hump on the other side. The earth spins, leaving the wave behind. As a consequence, we have the phenomenon of high and low water.

Let us not worry about friction, or about the amount the wave is retarded, or whether there is only one or a series of waves, or about what happens when the wave hits a continent, or whether the retarding effect of the wave is slowing down the rate of the earth's rotation, or the moon's. We will simply remember that the highest tides come one to three days after the full and the new moon, and are called "springs," and the lowest tides come when the moon is half-full—or at the quarter, in almanac terminology—and they are called "neaps." And we will also remember that about twelve hours elapse between tides, with the average daily progression in the time of high water being around fifty minutes (although it may vary from about thirty to eighty minutes).

Local tides at the shore depend upon the effect of shallow water contours on the tide wave. These may cause all kinds of queer local situations. However, as a result of careful recording, and with knowledge of the tide problem, accurate forecasts can be made for the future, not only in regard to the time of high water, but also in regard to the expected height of the tide. From such tide tables for the larger ports, tide in other areas can be computed by making a time allowance based on previous experience. These tables are surprisingly accurate, and we amateurs had best never doubt them.

The rise and fall of water—the tide, in other words—averages about four to five feet in the open ocean. The rise and fall is much modified in certain places. Increases occur as the result of the gradual confining of the tide wave into a narrowing funnel. At the head of the Bay of Fundy, a rise and fall of fifty feet is not unusual, sometimes on the flood accompanied by a four- or five-foot "bore," or water wall. On the contrary, the rise and fall in the Mediterranean tends to be very little—a foot and a half or so. At Boston, Massachusetts, the rise and fall varies from seven to eleven or more feet; in Buzzards Bay it is around four or five feet; while off our east beach at Eastham on Cape Cod, it is somewhere in between. The difference in time of high water between Boston Harbor and the Nauset Inlet is less than twenty minutes, while the difference between Boston and the head of Buzzards Bay is about three hours. When the Cape Cod Canal was built, it was freely predicted that it could not be worked without locks, in view of the three-hour difference in high water at the two ends. This prediction has proved to be near the truth. Not only does the swift current in the canal make its passage dangerous to shipping; but the current also constantly tends to wash away the shores and to fill in the channel, requiring a vast amount of riprapping as well as constant dredging.

One must bear in mind that "rise and fall" of the tide is not the same as "ebb and flow." Especially in estuaries and river mouths, the tide may begin to rise or fall an appreciable time before it begins to flood or ebb. I have frequently noticed this in the Nauset Marsh, where the early flood so often starts the flounders biting, or the ducks flying.

(Incidental note: The height of water over a bar at half tide will remain the same, regardless of the degree of rise and fall.)

In certain areas, "wind tides" are the important consideration. In the shallow sounds behind the Hatteras Beach, such as Currituck, Albemarle and Pamlico Sounds, "tides" are caused entirely by the winds. There are several small inlets, such as Oregon Inlet, which let enough salt water in to allow a fine type of eelgrass to grow in the vicinity, and, incidentally, brant to congregate, but these inlets have no appreciable effect on the rise and fall of the water. However, at Pea Island, a short distance south of Oregon Inlet, a fresh southwester might cause a rise of six or eight feet, and if continued would—and did—wash out the club house. Easterlies, on the other hand, result in the appearance of miles of sand flats. A man with great foresight built dykes, and trapped the high westerly tides, with the result that there is— or was, when I was there—a large area of fresh water ponds and fresh water grass, and consequent duck feed. This region has, I believe, been made into a federal game refuge.

The effect of tide on the solid, or semi-solid, earth is definite, but so small as to be negligible. It has been proposed that fresh-water fish are sensitive to the pull of earth and moon, the so-called "Solunar Theory." Elaborate tables have been developed, showing the times of best fishing. Some fishermen swear by these tables. As for me, I do not believe a word of it. So far, at least, no well-controlled experiments have been reported. Indeed, any well-controlled experiment would be extremely difficult to set up, in view of the great number of uncontrollable factors.

The tide inside our marsh is not easy to figure. This unusual marsh contains considerably more water than it does marsh land. The water part is supplied through a single narrow inlet, which varies greatly from year to year. Ten years ago, the Inlet was wide, the rise and fall considerable, with many flats and bars showing at low water. Today, the south shore of the Inlet has made way up by the north shore, to the northeast. As a result, there is little rise and fall, the water tends to remain at higher levels, and the flats either do not come out, or they stay out for only short periods. The immediate consequence of this is that the marsh is no longer a shore bird's paradise, but it may become more attractive to the ducks.

The flood inside the marsh takes from four to five hours, the ebb seven to eight hours. High water at the upper end (the Salt Pond Creek) is two and one-half to three hours later than high water on the outside. The result is quite extraordinary. Let us say the tide starts to flood on the outside at 8:00 A.M. It will be high outside about 2:00 P.M., and high in the Salt Pond Creek at 5:00 P.M. It will be low water in the Salt Pond Creek at 1:00 A.M. the next day, while high water outside will be but two hours later, at 3:00 A.M. In other words, the low water inside is within two hours of the high water outside. There are certain places, especially among islands, where ships can take advantage of a similar situation and have a constant fair tide through both flood and ebb. However that may be, the vagaries of the tide in the Nauset Marsh make difficult the figuring of the right time to go striped bass fishing—especially if you believe in Rule 357: "Striped bass tend to feed as the tide starts to ebb strongly"—or to hit that flat just in time to dig a mess of clams, or to "round the Horn" so as to meet the flood at the south end of the Porchy Marsh. In spite of many years' experience, one day last summer I found myself six hours out of the way!

The tide reams out channels. These gradually shift. I be-

lieve they go through regular cycles. I think the Inlet will close up as another inlet breaks through in the region of the Outermost House, to the north. This new inlet will gradually move southward until it reaches the present site. It cannot get further south because of the East Orleans headland. When and if a new inlet is formed, it will change the whole local picture.

I have watched channels inside the marsh go through several cycles. The Cedar Bank Channel, always so carefully guarded by my friend, the kingfisher, thirty-five years ago ran along the west side, leaving a hard sand bar to the east. Ten years later, it cut along the grass on the east bank. Gradually it worked west again for fifteen years and reached its original position. Then again it cut through at the east end, and is now about midway between. For how many centuries has this been going on? And how long will it continue?

Eelgrass may affect the tide. Channel grass tends to slow up the tide, resulting in the softening of the hard sand flats. This allows more grass to grow in, which may further slow up the tide. Possibly the contours of the marsh will markedly change in the next ten years.

In any case, tide greatly affects our lives. In general, low water provides the greatest interest. It is surprising how barren the marsh can become at the top of the tide. But paddle quietly down at low water, in early September, just before sunset, so that the sun is at your back. The flats will be covered with scurrying sandpipers of varying sizes. Trusting, black-bibbed ringnecks will solemnly eye you from a few feet as you drift past. The big yellowlegs will watch more warily, acknowledging your presence with an occasional formal bow, and will fly off suddenly, their flute-like call ringing loudly, their long yellow legs trailing behind. Or perhaps you will see the hunched-up, motionless dowitcher poking his long bill into the mud. Only if you are lucky will you find that stately king of the shore birds, the marbled godwit. But always something unusual, something interesting or new, will turn up, whether it be the great white egret, a pair of rare yellow-crowned night herons, an oyster catcher, a large lobster, or just the eel trap that rolled a long way upstream, due to the extra-strong flood tide.

And when the easterly storm strikes at the full of the moon, the marsh disappears from view, and a great sea takes its place. Woe to the gunner who tries to stick it out on top of the Middle Flat. He will soon find that 1.5 times the square root of the fetch will not only soak him through, but will also fill his boat. Hurry, hurry home, then, and get dry before that open fire, a steaming glass of grog in hand. Northeast storms are all right in their way, sometimes majestic in their fury, good for one's soul, and possibly necessary precursors to that sparkling nor'wester, but when they come, stay off that marsh!

18. Ice

WE MUST have had a series of cold Decembers when I was a boy. My first experiences with Cape Cod ice were at the Great Pond Camp over near the West Shore. Every Christmas vacation, so it seemed, we would find the Great Pond frozen over, and the problems and opportunities this presented would occupy most of our vacation time.

In the first place, if the ice were solid enough, pickerel traps always went up almost immediately, in the cove back of camp. At meal times a watch was kept from the living room window or from some other vantage point, and when a flag went up, great was the scramble to see who could arrive at the traps first. I don't think that the pounding over the ice did the fishing much good, but it was great fun, nevertheless.

Then there was skating. Usually the ice would be pretty rough, but once, I remember, the pond froze over in a sheet of absolutely smooth black ice. We enjoyed one day of gorgeous skating, and then, during the night, it rained. The next morning the ice was covered with about an inch of water. Some adventurous soul suggested skating just the same, and we found, to our delight, that the ice was as hard as ever. The water served only to reduce the friction. I came as close to flying like a bird as I ever have or probably ever will. It seemed to me that with just a tiny bit more effort I could have taken off and floated skyward across the pond. Of course, the inevitable occurred. I was gathering speed to accomplish a huge pigeonwing, which was to occupy about one half of the pond, when something happened. A skate slipped, perhaps *because* of the lack of friction, and I fell. I must have looked like a loon lighting, as spray shot up around my skidding form. I slid a hundred feet or more before coming to a stop, and, when I arose, I couldn't have been more thoroughly soaked had I jumped overboard in twenty feet of water.

With the pond frozen, we spent much time in keeping a hole open in front of the "blind." I had heard many tall stories about large bags of ducks shot over such a hole on previous occasions, but I myself never saw many ducks killed in this way—perhaps five or six in the course of a week, nothing more. I always have had rather an uncomfortable feeling shooting over an air hole. This never seemed to me to be giving the ducks a fair break. I suppose shooting from a blind might also have seemed unfair, but, as we did it, I never had this feeling about it.

I remember one night, at full moon, we watched the hole from sunset till midnight. During the day, we had sawed away great chunks of five-inch ice, and by stepping on one end, at great risk of a soaking, had slid them under the surface ice, thereby opening up a fair-sized hole. The thermometer, at twenty degrees above zero, was dropping rapidly, and only a strong northwest breeze kept the hole open. It was too cold for live decoys, and the wooden ones became iced up, and capsized. We put a few on the ice at the edge of the hole, and would have put out more, had we known better.

We stood at one of John's "stragic" points in the blind, where we could just see, above the brush that screened us, a huge orange moon rise rapidly, only to become smaller and smaller, and more and more brittle, until finally it seemed as if a light tap would shatter it into a thousand pieces. It was cold there, in spite of our being fairly well protected from the wind. I don't think we would have stuck it out if John hadn't told us about a similar night when he and another had shot twenty black ducks.

But by far the most impressive thing about it was listening to the straining complaint of the ice itself. Owing to the rapidly dropping temperature, the ice was continually contracting, and this appeared to make it suffer terribly. Way down toward the east end would start a vague noise. Rapidly it would travel up to the west, gaining momentum and volume, until, as it passed us, the boom and crack resembled nearby thunder. Then, gradually waning, it would run on across, and subside on the west shore of the pond.

It is impossible to describe the awesome fullness of this sound. It made us, my friend and me, feel as if the world were coming apart at the seams. Every once in a while, one of these opening cracks would seem to be coming directly for us, and unconsciously we would brace ourselves for the shock. Brrr-ump! Brrrr-ump! Boom! Boom! BOOM! it would go, as it passed by us.

We could not imagine that any self-respecting black duck would subject himself to such terrifying sounds, but, along about ten o'clock, we suddenly saw two black things at the ice edge which had not been there before. We shot at the count, and slaughtered two ducks. These were the only birds we saw. Thoroughly chilled, we went back to the house about midnight, with the moon now high overhead, and toasted ourselves in front of the dying embers of a huge fire.

Salt ice is a different proposition. In the first place, it is treacherous. You may be walking over it, confident of a solid thickness beneath your feet, when suddenly, without warning, you go plunging down through. The story that someone drove across Buzzards Bay from Marion in a horse-drawn buggy makes me shudder.

On the West Shore at Eastham, ice behaves in a very peculiar way. The West Shore flats come out at low water for a mile or more. In a winter nor'wester, as the tide floods, a considerable sea develops—not a real surf, but good heavy waves. If the temperature is down around fifteen degrees above zero or so, the sea water drops below its freezing temperature of about twenty-seven degrees. The result is that the water becomes thick with what is locally known as "slur." (The only definition of "slur" I can find that is at all applicable is "thin, watery mud.") This slur piles up higher and higher on the beach and extends further and further offshore, until only a shallow crescent of deep blue, far out beyond the white, indicates open water.

It is a magnificent sight when this occurs, but let anyone who tries to traverse this ice beware! The slur freezes up, sometimes so solidly that you can walk on top of it. Suddenly, however, the surface film gives way, and you fall through an air-filled, flaky mass that has little substance. Since there is no way of telling how thick the frozen layer is, nor how much water there is beneath, it is a hazardous procedure indeed to walk over it. Even if the flats are out, you can fall into a pocket six feet deep or more in slur ice and have trouble getting out again.

Sometimes a spring or creek will melt a canyon through the ice until it reaches open water. But even here it is not too safe to walk at low water. As the tide floods, the mouth may become plugged with freezing slur, only to give way suddenly as the pressure becomes too great. Then he who has ventured down the canyon must turn and run for his life, pursued by a real bore of ice, slush, and water three or four feet high.

But it is on the Nauset Marsh, on the east side of the Cape, that I have had most of my experiences with salt ice, and very

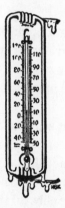

bitter some of them have been. The process of the solid freezing-up of the marsh is interesting to watch, but, to get the feel of it, one must be right there amongst it. Only a strong urge to hunt would cause an otherwise apparently sane individual to subject himself to the suffering it entails.

Cold fronts, of course, are very frequently accompanied by strong northwest winds. With the thermometer at fifteen degrees or below, and with a near-gale blowing out of the northwest, duck shooting from a gunning float is far from easy. No amount of clothing seems to shut out the chill; mittens are always inadequate and are bound to get wet. To be sure, real fishermen's mittens are only warm when wet, but to take out a wet hand, as is frequently necessary in order to shoot, simply intensifies the bitter cold. Oars become greasy with ice, and, when pulled upon, frequently jump out of their locks. Salt spray freezes where it hits, and, should the safety catch of your gun become frozen, it must be thawed, perhaps with your bare hand. Decoys become iced up and top-heavy, and soon capsize. The water bottle freezes, but no one wants water. If you have been brave enough to light a pipe, the juice in the stem freezes and plugs the pipe up even while it is going. Looking into the wind makes your face ache, and prevents watering eyes from seeing. And those feet, so far away from warm heart's blood! How they ache and ache, until a blessed numbness warns of impending danger.

As the tide drops, the water becomes thicker and thicker. Wherever there is a lee, the slur shows white, and little griddlecakes of ice gradually appear, growing constantly larger. Shortly, they begin to coalesce until a large cake has been formed. As the tide ebbs off the flats, these cakes rapidly become heavier and stronger. Meanwhile, back on the marsh, the pud-holes solidly freeze over, and ice crystals shine on the grass stems where the tide has dropped off.

Now comes the flood, and, with it, chunks of ice which have been lifted off the flats. You must keep a wary eye out, lest suddenly the whole caboodle of your decoys should start upstream at an incredible speed, carried by the irresistible surge of the ice. Quickly the boat is hauled out, but the ice interferes with rowing. Lucky you are if you can reach bottom to pole. When finally the decoys are rescued, it is a long trek back to get the rest of the gear. Keep, then, close to the sedge, from which, if necessary, the boat can be dragged through the ice.

The sensible thing to do is to come home, but possibly you have found a little backwater, free from floe ice. Here you may be secure for a time, with only the difficult and sometimes dangerous task of retrieving your game to worry you. Also, as the flood increases, the warmer water from the ocean will tend to melt the ice a little and prevent, for a time, further caking. However, you are beginning to wonder about negotiating the upper channels. There's that place off Hay Island, you remember, into which cake ice tends to jam. Once it does, it won't be long before the channel is solidly plugged. And what about that warm fire in the Farm House living room?

There comes a moment when your only thought is of getting back, and this is the coldest time of all. You get up from the shelter of your boat, and the icy wind reaches into your bones. Numb hands take in the tangled decoys. Finally, all is stowed away, and you start the row back. In a surprisingly short time, a delicious warmth begins to permeate your entire body. Returning circulation brings a peculiarly pleasurable pain to fingers and toes. The upper channels are *not* plugged, and the flooding tide counteracts the force of the head wind. Before you know it, you find yourself at the boathouse, standing in its lee and enjoying a respite from the tearing wind. Better untangle the decoys now; tomorrow they will be a frozen mess.

Next day, the bay below the hill and the West Cove are a solid sheet of white ice. Except for a little open water here and there, the channel is plugged as far down as the Cedar Bank. Had you been planning to go shooting, you would have done well to leave your boat there last night.

By the following night, the nor'wester has blown itself out. The air is still and very cold. Now, at low tide, what open water there is will skim over with a quarter inch of ice, and, with no wind and cake ice to break it up, it will thicken and solidify. After a third day of intense cold, the marsh will be frozen tight, except perhaps for an air hole just by the Porchy Bar, and maybe another in the Beach Channel, just above Caleb's Hummock. Gunning now becomes hazardous in the extreme. The main point is to avoid deep water. This involves an accurate knowledge of tides and channels, and, in any case, is not always possible. We carry special ice picks tied with a single twist around our necks, so that in an emergency we can pull ourselves out on the ice.

With the boat on solid ice, you man the drag ropes at the forward end of the cockpit and drag the boat, at not too great labor, along the surface. If the ice gives way, you throw yourself across the forward deck, and, although you may go in up to your shoulders, if you scramble out quickly, your inner clothing may not get wet.

Should the boat be in the water to start with, the process is quite complicated but not too difficult if bottom can be reached with an oar. With the weight aft, the boat is put up onto the ice as far as she will go. Then one man gets astride the bow, and puts his weight on the ice. If it gives way, he sits down on the deck and the other man poles or sculls the boat forward. If the ice doesn't give way, the bow man gets out on it and heaves on a towline short enough so that he can get back on the deck again if necessary. Then, very gingerly, the other man gets out, and both take the drag ropes and again start off. This process may have to be repeated three or four times before the air hole is reached.

Another method is for one man to walk along the edge of the sedge with a long towline, pulling the boat after him, while the second man pushes with an oar against the forward oarlock post, thus keeping the boat away from the marsh. However, numerous creeks, always treacherous to cross, cause much trouble. Neither method classifies as light work.

When the air hole is reached, the shooting is likely to be good, the hole being one of the few places where food is available. But, as I have said before, it bothers my conscience to shoot ducks under such circumstances. All in all, I would just as soon not have the marsh freeze up, or, if it does, I would rather be there when it lets go.

This it does with miraculous rapidity. Comes a night when the sky will be filled with too many stars, and, the next day, a rapidly thickening smur will obscure the sunlight. By nightfall, the wind will freshen from the southeast as the thermometer starts to climb. At midnight, it will blow a gale, driving a heavy rain through the south window frames.

Twelve hours later, the wind has dropped and the sky cleared. Take an observation now from the top of the hill. Lo and behold! The channels are open. Only the protected bays, like Nauset Bay and West Cove, contain solid ice. Here and there a white patch will shine out from the top of the marsh, where last night's high tide has carried a floe of ice.

"Hurrah!" you exclaim. "Tomorrow we can row where we want to and not be bothered by ice."

But your triumph is apt to be short-lived. Tomorrow brings another nor'wester, and again the thermometer tumbles. Again the ice begins to make, and likely the next day the fight begins all over. As the winter advances, especially if it is a hard winter, the marsh may be frozen up most of the time.

Yes, it's a grand sight to look out over the frozen marsh from the top of the Cedar Bank, the large blocks of white ice sharply outlined against the dark sedge, with perhaps here and there a spot of bright blue water. As I grow older, however, I'm inclined to let it go at that. The Farm House is almost as nice to get back to after a brisk walk in a fresh nor'-wester, as it is after a fight with the ice—and you're not too exhausted to enjoy it.

19. The March Doldrums

IT IS not mentioned in any classified list of medical diseases, but it is nevertheless a very common complaint. I call it the "March Doldrums." The symptoms are varied, and there is no clear textbook description which will fit all cases. The victim is apt to be even more querulous than usual; he swears at his family when he cannot find his hat, on the mistaken theory that someone has given it away, and then finds that, having forgotten to take it off when he came in, he left it hanging on a nail by the coal bin; he yells, in uncomplimentary language, at the driver of the car behind who insists on continuously blowing his horn, in spite of the fact that there is a ten-ton truck-trailer jackknifed across the highway; and, in general, he displays unseemly behavior. He is probably overweight, has a pasty complexion, and coughs continually. His work is a bore, hardly worth the effort, and his boss is losing his grip. In short, the March Doldrums sufferer is in a very sorry state.

The treatment is simple. Ten days' stay at the Farm House, say in late March or early April, will produce a cure in one hundred per cent of cases. It is hardly even necessary to administer penicillin.

It is cold on Cape Cod in March. We have a late spring, two or three weeks later than Boston. This is due to the fact that we are almost completely surrounded by the sea. Water neither absorbs nor radiates heat as rapidly as does the solid land and therefore water maintains a much more constant temperature. It takes the sea longer to cool off and longer to warm up; consequently, the fall season at the Farm House is warmer, and the spring season colder, than further inland. In late March or the first week in April, the temperature is likely to be around thirty degrees in the morning, and often does not rise above forty, even when the sun is high. The wind almost always blows "right pert," generally from a northerly quarter. Dry northeasters, of which I have previously written, are the season's specialty.

There is no shooting, all kinds of game being protected by law. Striped bass do not appear until May. "Skittering" for pickerel, a fine sport involving the use of a long bamboo pole and a minnow, is now prohibited in March and April, when this fish is spawning. One can catch flounder, but this is devilishly cold work, and, when indulged in, denotes a condition bordering on starvation. True, in 1945 and 1946, we did have a week of extraordinarily warm weather, the thermometer on one occasion rising to within peeking distance of eighty, and on these two trips we had some real fun flounder fishing. At this time of year, they run large and produce delicious fillets if properly prepared. (I have, after great travail, more or less learned how to "skiver" a flounder, but some of us still use the "blanching" technique, whereby the flounder is scalded for about seven seconds in boiling water, after which the skin can easily be teased off.)

As a rule, however, at this time of year there are no major activities, which is a good thing for the Doldrum patient. He is under no pressure, can sleep as he pleases, and need hardly stick his nose out of the house if he does not wish to. Nevertheless, if he gets just one sniff of Eastham air, carried to him off the ocean by a fresh northeast breeze, the chances are that he will soon begin to stir his stumps, take longer and longer walks, until, towards the end of the trip, he thinks nothing of a ten- or twelve-mile hike.

I do not know what it is about the air here at Eastham that makes it so different. I have heard many people speak of the exhilarating mountain air, and I will admit that the cool nights of mountain climates are refreshing. Our Cape air has a positive element that gives one the effect of tasting or ingesting something delicious and life-giving. Those who, in summer, complain of being let down by it, have missed the significant point. They have been traveling at too rapid a pace, and they are fortunate indeed if they can expose themselves to the healing qualities of this Cape Cod atmosphere. Call it sparkling, clean, clear, pure, champagne-like—or what you will; it has a quality that is indescribable. And the time one needs it most is at the end of a long winter.

At this time of year, we like to visit the "back side" ponds. Off to the northeast of the Farm House the country consists of rolling hills interspersed with sharp little hollows, each one of which contains some water. Most of them are surrounded by pitch pines, but the ridges are often clear, except for a bronzed carpet of bearberry, dotted here and there with a dark oval patch of a foot-high, springy bush. We call it "couch bush," so comfortable is it to lie upon. In some areas, scrub oak is mixed with the pine, making travel difficult. Indeed, further to the north, between Nauset Light and the North Eastham railroad station, there is a large tract of almost solid scrub oak which is very nearly impassable. Only by crawling on hands and knees along deer trails, which here are as numerous, narrow, and exasperating as the streets of Boston, can one get through. I know, because I have done it. Nice judgment is required in picking the trail which will lead in the right direction, and, what with the twisting and turning, together with the dim light due to the overhead tangle of branches still holding oak leaves, one's sense of direction becomes severely taxed. A compass is a comforting thing to have under such circumstances.

It is usually about half past ten by the Farm House clock, by the time we get started. We have had a leisurely breakfast and a leisurely cleanup. The thermometer has risen to thirty-six degrees from its low of twenty-eight. The wind is fresh northeast, the sky clear and as blue as blue can be. We wear what seems like less clothing than the situation demands, for we have learned by experience that one must begin by feeling cold, if one wishes to avoid the bother later on of having to carry cast-off windbreakers.

Commonly, we start off on the same route as the one we

take when walking down the beach—that is, down by the pond back of the barn and then along the Cedar Bank to the Quawkery at the head of Nauset Bay. Here we branch off to the north, and follow a pebbly, little-used road through the woods. One can travel very silently over this track, provided one is not conversationally minded, and, as a consequence, we sometimes come close upon a deer. We stand perfectly still, and, for a while, the deer, being upwind, also stands motionless, his huge ears cocked and his prominent dark eyes filled with a mixture of curiosity and fear. Some one of our party makes an unintended motion, and away goes the deer in a series of effortless leaps. The last we see of him is his erect white tail as it disappears into the scrub. One always reads of the deer's "spring-like" legs, or legs of "sinewed steel," and such things. The impression I get is that the deer has chosen to light upon springs hidden in the ground, which propel him upwards and forwards, and which require practically no action on his part.

We soon leave the road and cut across country into the "wilderness." First we skirt Single Snipe Pond, a grassy little pond often just shallow and muddy enough to attract snipe. Before the great freeze, involving the whole southern seaboard about 1938, snipe were fairly common in late September and October, and tradition has it that this pond always held one snipe—just one.

About two hundred yards to the north of Single Snipe Pond is Round Pond. If you come upon it from the high ridge to the east, you look down on an absolutely round pond, scarcely sixty yards across. It is surrounded by a fringe of low shrubs, such as black alder and high-bush blueberry, while further back there is a smattering of young pitch pines six to eight feet high. The water, on such a day as this, is riffled by the fresh breeze and its color is the purest blue that can be imagined.

Generally, however, we approach Round Pond from the west, where there is a cover of pines and shrubs. We walk up very slowly, single file, placing our feet with great care. Woe unto him who causes a twig to snap! For one never knows what Round Pond may have in store.

Once, we peeked out from behind a pine and saw five pairs of green-winged teal. The male greenwing is as handsome a bird as one could wish to see. After some minutes of observation, during which the teal were completely unaware of our presence, it became apparent that one of the males was different from the others. He lacked the white crescent which dips down below the waterline just forward of the wing, and he had a white streak down each side of his back. It was a European teal, of exceedingly rare occurrence. Curiously enough, on this same day some four hours later, a European teal was observed near Newburyport, Massachusetts, perhaps sixty air miles away. I like to think that this bird was working his way northeastward toward his breeding grounds.

We have watched unsuspecting pintails at close range, seen hooded mergansers and pied-billed grebes, mallards, and other, for us, unusual species, but it is rare indeed that we can observe black ducks here. We often come almost upon them, but they sense our presence before we see them, and the first we know of them is the crash of their jump and the rush of their wings. That "Grand Old Man of the Marshes," the great blue heron, sometimes comes to Round Pond to look for frogs, but he, too, is seldom caught napping. And in August, if the water level is right, the sweet-scented white water lily will be in full bloom. I have seen these flowers in great profusion elsewhere, but they never seem so beautiful as they do lying on the surface of this little pond.

From Round Pond, we strike out over the ridge to the northeast. As we pass a long, nameless pond, a large, shadowy bird silently slips out of a tree, sails across the pond and disappears. He makes us shiver a little, for we know he is the Big Owl, the great horned owl. He it is who has cleaned the night herons out of the Quawkery and made the crows change their roosting place. And he it is whose calls we may hear even from the Farm House. Sometimes they remind us of a dog barking; but at closer range there is a vibrant quality to the note, a wildness to it, something untrammeled and limitless, which both thrills and frightens us.

Our next stop is Mayflower Pond. One must know exactly where to go to find mayflowers, and they do not stand injudicious picking. I would not mention them here if I thought that anyone could possibly find Mayflower Pond from my description. I do not worry, however, because there is considerable doubt in my mind as to my own family's ability to find it.

Mayflower Pond is really only a puddle, and a small one at that. It is about ten or twelve feet across, at most. We reach it by pushing through the thick pines and some scrub oak, just northwest of the long, Horned Owl Pond. If we have made the proper calculations, we suddenly find ourselves by a grassy pool situated in a little dip in the pine forest. It is completely sheltered from all winds, and the sun beats down on its south bank with an inviting warmth. Look closely among the old leaves on this side, and under them you will soon find patches of mayflower plants. Lift up a sprig, and underneath you will find a cluster of buds with, at this time of year, just a bit of white showing. With luck, you will find one or two which have taken on a glorious pink color. There is something about this color which is absolutely soul-satisfying. The mayflower—modest, beautiful and joyous—I believe to be the finest of all flowers.

Mayflower Pond calls for a fifteen-minute rest. Some lie on the ground on their backs and look up into the blue of the sky; some strip to the waist and allow the sun's warm rays to rejuvenate their skin; and some squat at the pond's edge to see what life it may hold. Stay here, perfectly still, and watch. After a long while, you notice little bubbles which keep coming to the surface, and as quickly disappear. After some time, you are fascinated to discover that these are not bubbles at all. They are the noses and eyes of tiny frogs. If you are not by now too cramped, stay perfectly still a while longer. You may be rewarded by seeing a frog, hardly three quarters of an inch long, climb out onto a spear of grass, clinging to it by means of the suckers on his toes. These suckers proclaim him to be one of the tree-frog family, the *Hyla*, and he is the smallest of all our frogs. Like many of the hylas, he has on his back a dark and somewhat wavering cross.

As you watch the little fellow, the underside of his mouth becomes enormously distended. The shrill note that suddenly erupts is so startlingly loud, almost ear-piercing, that you involuntarily straighten up, whereat he disappears as if by magic, as do all the little bubbles. This song of the spring peeper (technically known as *Hyla pickeringi* or *Hyla crucifer*) is well recognized as a joyous overture to

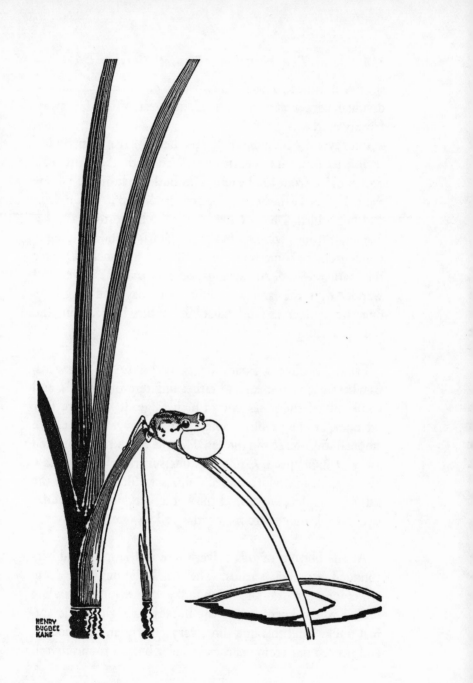

HENRY
BUGBEE
KANE

spring. It is not so well known that one may hear an individual peeper at any time of the year, often far away from water.

On several occasions in September, I have spent hours trying to find and identify the bird with the shrill call which came from the beach-plum bush back of the woodshed. It was years before I discovered that it was a frog and not a bird. I have once in a while heard the call of a peeper, during winter thaws in January and February, coming out of some pool where the ice had melted. After the mating season, the spring peepers leave the water and wander over the land. On some moist day you may hear one, and wonder, as I did, what kind of bird is producing the sound.

From Mayflower Pond, we work off to the eastward, pass between two small and rather uninteresting ponds, and climb out of the pines onto a high ridge. It was here that we once, at close range, came upon a very yellow cat. We stopped still, and so did the cat. Then he turned and bounded away at high speed. Great was our surprise when we saw his long, bushy, white-tipped tail. As we dropped over the side of the ridge, we started another larger and much redder fox. I think they were mates, the yellow one probably the vixen.

At the bottom of this ridge, there is a larger pond surrounded by thick shrubs. There is only one spot from which one can examine this pond, and it requires crawling on hands and knees below the bushes through a little animal track. I did this one time, very quietly and cautiously, and peeked out from beneath an alder bush. I found myself looking a black duck in the eye at a range of four feet. I think this is the nearest I have ever been to a wild black duck, and it gave me quite a start. Even then, the duck, though becoming slightly suspicious, only slid offshore a short distance and continued to eye me curiously. We stared at each other for a while, neither one seeming to be quite willing to make the first move. Finally, I slowly moved back and succeeded in leaving without flushing him.

However, when we followed the path around the north end of the pond, still completely hidden, there was a great commotion as fifteen black ducks and eight geese, none of which had I seen, struggled straight up in the air in order to gain sufficient elevation to clear the trees. Some say that ducks have a well-developed olfactory sense, and that they will detect man's presence by such means. This I do not believe. I know that they have an acute sense of hearing, and in this instance I think they heard some sound when we came dead to windward.

From here, the trail winds around through a solid stand of old pitch pines. These pines are not very tall, but they are as tall as any around here, with the possible exception of those to the north of the Great Pond. Once we flushed a great horned owl from a nest at the top of one of these trees. This nest was not large, as many of them are, and consisted of a bunch of small twigs put together in what seemed a very flimsy fashion. We thought of climbing the tree to see the young, which, in March, should have been there, but we were deterred by those stories about fierce horned owls attacking people who ventured too close to their offspring-filled nests.

At last we climb a steep rise and leave the woods behind

us. Another half mile through beach grass and bayberry, interspersed with dense clumps of low scrub oaks, and we reach the edge of the cliffs. To the north is Nauset Light, its tall red and white tower replacing the original three lights, while to the south, on a low hill, stands the Nauset Coast Guard Station, its weather vane still twisted so that the "N" points to the south. Below us is the beach, very white in the bright light, bathed in a wash of foam, and stretching to north and south as far as the eye can reach.

And there before us is the great ocean. Today its color is a deep blue, except alongshore, where the shallow, sandy bottom gives it a greenish cast. The stiff northeast wind has caused a jumble of waves and plenty of white water. The horizon is sharp, except for the lumpiness of the sea, and, off to the southeast, a freighter, hull down, can just be made out. The breeze is cool, almost cold, and feels delightfully refreshing after our almost too warm walk through the woods. It carries with it a distinct aroma; it has body, and a tangy taste that reminds me of the quality of certain wines. Physical fatigue is dissipated, mental strain and stress retreat into the far background, and a sense of proportion and balance returns. Those affairs that you, and only you, could have dealt with do not now seem so important; perhaps, after all, someone else will do them better. It is a joy to be alive and, for the moment, this is all that matters.

We rest for a few minutes and scan the sea with our glasses. There is a small bunch of eiders off the Coast Guard Station, a few coots or scoters, directly offshore, and, in close, a red-throated loon, identified by his bill, which seems to have a slight upward curve. (It is not really curved, however; the upper mandible is almost straight and the lower one has a normal curve. This, together with the bird's tendency to tip his bill slightly upward, gives an illusion of an actual upward curve.) In the distance, we can pick up with the glasses three or four gannets, looking very white in the bright sunlight. On the whole, however, we find little bird life of any great interest, and the breeze becomes almost too cold. We turn our backs to it and head for home.

The walk back is not difficult. We may skirt the woods, cross the road, and retrace our steps by the Quawkery and along the Cedar Bank. Or, if we are tired, we may follow the road all the way. Or we may make a compromise and leave the road at the big rock—the Minister's Rock—from whose top one car get a wide view of the marsh and the surrounding country. In any case, at last we find ourselves in the hollow, trudging through the low blackberry or thimbleberry vines. Better be wearing thick socks or high boots, else you will get badly scratched, even if you have learned to do the Cape Cod "backward kick" before advancing your rear foot. The climb up the hill is just as hard as ever, and the reward just as great. For there at the top is the Farm House, waiting to greet you.

Gone now are the March Doldrums. All mental cobwebs have been swept away, hearty laughter has replaced quavering complaint, that pasty look has given way to a ruddy complexion and a clear eye, and the belt is buckled at a more normal and healthy spot. Yes, the March Doldrums is a serious and common disease, which, fortunately, is easily treated. However, before treatment can be applied, the diagnosis must be made. It is a pity that so often it remains unrecognized either by doctor or by patient.

20. Bird Flight

OWING to the development of high-speed cameras, the problems involving bird flight are becoming better understood. From inspection of photographs, it would seem that birds do not simply row through the air. In fact, on the down beat, the wings are actually brought forward. If the bird were "rowing," he would necessarily travel stern first, a feat that only the hummingbird is good at. It appears that the wing action is more comparable to the action of an airplane propeller than to an oar. This, in part, is due to an extraordinarily rapid back flip of the wing, especially at the "wrist," on its upward thrust. Farther than this I cannot go. However, I want particularly to talk about bird flight as observed by the naked eye, not infrequently aided by a pair of 8 x 40 binoculars.

Gulls—sea gulls, or more accurately, herring gulls—are, I think, the laziest birds in the world, or at least in New England. The herring gull will never make an unavoidable wingbeat. He will even neglect to take his nightly flight to his roost if the air is still and heavy; especially is this true if there is a light fog. One evening last summer, just at sunset, I saw a few herring gulls slowly winging their way to the west toward their night roost on Jeremy Point or the Billingsgate Island Bar. They seemed to bob up and down as, with obvious effort, wingbeat followed wingbeat. It was no surprise to me when, along about midnight, as we were trying to catch a striped bass for our next day's dinner, we ran into swads of herring gulls sitting out the calm night on the Goose Hummock flats.

But take a dry northeaster with the rising sun, when freed of cloud, warming the land. Gulls are making their way back to the marshes as the ebb clears the flats. They do not fly. They soar and sail, go ten miles off their course to gain a favorable air current, luff up sharply, and rise to the unexpected catspaw, then scale down at an angle into the wind eddy below the hill, an occasional lazy downthrust of wing the only sign of expended energy. Or later on, when the wind has dropped, they will circle higher and higher, carried up by rising air, until they become scarcely distinguishable against the sky. Often this seems to be only for enjoyment, but sometimes they take off on a slow glide for some distant source of nourishment.

We have other gulls: the great black-backed gull, that vicious marauder who, in his adult plumage, stands proudly on the Teal Hummock flat, dressed in black dinner coat and stiff white shirt, and fights off all and sundry who dispute his domain; the laughing gull, with his derisive cry, who frequently depends on others to provide his dinner; and the modest, better-groomed counterpart of his herring-gull cousin, the ring-billed gull, only recently established here from more westerly areas.

The terns, commonly called mackerel gulls, are, of course, entirely different in their behavior. Full of nervous energy, they are always on the move, now flying directly, with powerful strokes, toward a distantly spied flock of their brethren who have found fish, now diving headlong with half-folded wing, or cruising in abrupt circles, bill down and eyes on the water. Every so often, one or two will light on a lobster buoy, or perhaps in a compact flock they will settle on a sand bar or sand flat, and rest without movement.

Sometimes on a still, warm September day, the terns may be seen flying high in irregular circles and making sudden dips. A sharp eye and a good glass will disclose that they are after flying ants which have chosen that day for their nuptial performance. Frequently, the terns are joined by laughing gulls and herring gulls, and I have even seen a winter yellowlegs following their lead. This habit seems peculiar as only the black tern is normally a bug-eater.

An exciting and rather terrifying experience is a visit to a nesting colony such as used to occur on Tern Island in the Nauset Marsh. Here, one's world is limited by a swirl of screaming terns. Here, from among the shifting snow-white storm of wings and sharp forked tails, one may in time distinguish the more stately arctic tern from its close relative, the common tern. The rare, large, gull-sized Caspian tern may possibly be seen, and the tiny, over-energetic least tern, now more and more abundant, will be fussing and fidgeting among his bigger cousins. One will be glad of a stout hat, for many a diving tern comes within inches of one's head. It is said they actually strike people who invade their privacy.

Among the fastest fliers is the teal. Many a gunner has watched a teal skip in and out among his decoys before a shot was possible. Frequently, a single teal will jump into the air from a marsh puddle, and join, with no apparent effort, a flock of black ducks passing a hundred yards overhead. They have been clocked at ninety to one hundred twenty miles per hour. It is well for them that they are so speedy, for they are overly trusting of man, and have even visited, on occasion, the puddle back of the barn.

Each species of duck has a characteristic flight. In general, the diving duck's flight is more direct and faster-winged than that of his more leisurely and graceful relatives, the river and pond ducks. Such birds as the scoter, or coot, and eider, or sea duck, give the impression of great weight and flying effort. They usually fly low and do not deviate from their course, whereas such species as the black duck

or the pintail fly high, their course unpredictable, and their speed and manner of flight varying greatly.

My favorite, of course, is the black duck. I still get the "prickles" when, out of the night, from well overhead comes the high-pitched whistling of a black duck's wings. This whistling, by the way, is a common characteristic of most ducks, reaching its peak in the male goldeneye, or "whistler," whose musical whistle on a still morning can be heard a long distance. Many a night have I lain in a boat, shivering and half frozen, listening to passing wings. Suddenly there would be a loud tearing sound, a "whoosh" of wings, and a splash. I would know there was a duck among my decoys, but the darkness would hide him. Sometimes I might find him in the light of setting Venus—my night vision used to be amazingly good—but more often I would flush him out when at last the cold became unbearable.

Black ducks normally fly at about forty miles per hour, though they may reach sixty. They do not appear to have great difficulty in winds of ordinary force, such as gales up to forty or forty-five miles per hour. In full gales of sixty

miles or so, they have real trouble. In such cases, I have frequently seen them tack their way to windward in long hitches. Sometimes they will gain a hundred yards, sometimes none at all. I have never seen them in winds of hurricane force, that is, seventy-five miles per hour and over. I did see winter yellowlegs try to make to windward against the southeast hurricane of 1938. However, we at Eastham were only on the edge of it, and the estimated velocity was not over seventy-five miles per hour. The yellowlegs took three long tacks and gained about a hundred yards. At this point they lit, apparently content to wait it out.

With apologies to the golden plover, it is my belief that the most spectacular bird in flight is the peregrine, or duck hawk. One day in mid-October 1945, I was lying with a friend in a duckboat. This is the season of greatest duck-hawk abundance on the Nauset Marsh. As the flats began coming out they were soon covered with shore birds, mostly red-backed sandpipers, with a sprinkling of yellowlegs and black-bellied plover. We soon knew there was a duck hawk around, for, of a sudden, preceded by a peculiarly shrill call, every shore bird on the marsh was in the air. Flocks of four or five hundred sandpipers turned and twisted in the sunlight, now light, now dark, as if a light switch had been turned on and off. Incidentally, the camera might show the answer to the query: how do sandpipers turn all at the same time? Do they actually "follow the leader," but too fast for human eye to see, or do they have some sense of the rhythm of flight, similar to that of dancers?

On the day in question, we were set with our duck decoys in a small puddle surrounded by flats, and it so happened that we were right in line with the duck hawk's favorite pitch. We saw him soaring in tight circles, reaching skyward with unbelievable speed and drifting to the east before a fresh westerly breeze. At this particular moment there was but a single sandpiper around, about fifty yards in front of us. Finally the hawk became an almost invisible speck, but with his keen eye apparently still focussed on the unsuspecting red-back. Then down he plunged in a near-vertical dive. He drove past us at grass-top level, within fifteen feet, so fast we could hardly follow him. At this point the peep saw him and jumped. When two feet from the ground, and just as the hawk got there, the peep made a right-angle turn. The hawk turned also, with a searing, tearing crash of sound—but too late. Then back and forth, up and down and around they went, until the hawk tired of the chase. Up, up, up he went, and in a matter of seconds disappeared into the blue.

The flying ability of my friend the crow has been much underrated. Because of his rather broad, blunt wings, he has been accused of being clumsy, and no one thinks of him as an expert flier. Yet the crow is one of the fastest, most efficient fliers there are. The expression "as the crow flies" is a good one. No dillydallying, no tacking and gliding for the crow; he takes off for his destination, goes by the shortest possible route, and wastes no time about it. I have often watched crows, making for their roost, flying into a brisk head wind. They do not appear to be effective as they flap, flap their way into the wind. But just look at your watch and see how long it takes them. I have surprised many a crow among the cedars of the Cedar Bank, and I know of no bird that can make a quicker getaway. Only the other day, I saw a crow take off from a cedar tree and rapidly overtake an eagle, who was vainly trying to escape by soaring into the sky. In a matter of seconds the crow had overtaken the eagle and was badgering him from above.

The hovering habit identifies certain birds almost at once. The "hoverers" maintain a constant position in the air by rapid wing action. One of these is the pretty little chestnut-backed, insect-eating falcon, the sparrow hawk. His characteristic pose is in a fixed position over the brow of a hill where he may be seen rapidly beating his wings to sustain himself over some hidden succulent morsel. Other hawks do the same thing, the rough-legged hawk, for one. I have also watched the red-tailed hawks, hunting for mice, take to this motion, especially when they had young in the nest, but this is unusual. And, of course, the fish hawk, or osprey, the only bird I know of that catches fish in his talons, will hover for long periods before making his breath-taking plunge.

There is one more hoverer to mention, the kingfisher. Almost any day, you can find him on the peak of the boat-house roof, or atop the post by the creek. He may make a sudden dash from his perch, or may hover over a shallow beach. Suddenly he smacks into the water with a great splash, a belly-flopper if there ever was one. And for good reason, too, for he takes his prey from an inch of water, where the tern, if he had dived, would have broken his neck. The cheery, rattling call of the friendly kingfisher is a necessary part of our Farm House life.

And what about the worst of our local fliers, the rail? Many times, while tramping swampy, fresh-water meadows, I have jumped rails, usually soras or Virginias. With what seems like the most stupendous effort, they flutter along for perhaps fifty feet, and drop, apparently exhausted, into the grass. Try as you will—stamp back and forth, crisscross, and circle—you cannot make the bird take to the air again. No wonder the tradition grew up of the rail's ride south on the back of the crane. How else could such a weak flier escape the rigors of a New England winter? It was seriously proposed that gallinules, close relatives of the rails, migrated by running overland. However, the lighthouse keeper on Billingsgate Island, when I was a boy, brought me a dead gallinule. The bird had broken its neck by flying against the light. There can be no doubt that gallinules and rails, in spite of their clumsy flying, migrate north and south in the air, and very likely at great altitude.

Gannets, on the other hand, are superb flyers. In April or November they are commonly seen off the Nauset Beach. They seem to like best a fresh breeze and a long, heavy sea. With outstretched wing, a magnificent white against the blue ocean, they will coast up over the crest of a wave, rise a few feet, and slide gracefully down into the trough with hardly a wing motion. When fishing, they circle at a higher level, stop suddenly, and then dive, straight and true, head down, wings partly shut. A four-foot geyser marks their contact with the water. Five to seven seconds later they reappear, shake themselves, and slowly take to the air to try again.

Once I saw a flock of about two thousand gannets, all fishing. This was off Oregon Inlet on the Hatteras Beach. The birds had discovered a school of small fish, possibly mullets, which were being harried by larger fish below. The sun was shining brightly, and was not too high. The birds in the forward edge of the flock were all dropping out of the air into a smother of spray; as they reappeared, the flock had passed by, and they joined the rear, soon to reach the lead again. It was a waterfall of gleaming white birds against a background of gentian blue water.

I have written of birds and their flying. Let experts take photographs, perhaps with high-speed cameras. From them we will learn much. But let us, you and I, just go outdoors and watch the birds fly.

21. Bird Language

THE subject of bird language has often been discussed, frequently with a good deal of heat. At one time, it was fashionable to deride the notion that birds might have a language of their own. The thought long held sway that most bird song, as distinguished from call notes, was strictly a courtship performance, but recently it has been realized more and more that song may also be used to establish the boundaries of a breeding territory. From my own observations, I believe that bird notes can be divided into several categories:

1. Chatter, such as humans indulge in at teas or cocktail parties.
2. Discussion of plans, such as might occur at a board meeting.
3. Maintenance of contact, such as the whistling of one partridge hunter to another in order that the proper position may be kept, and accidents avoided.
4. Warning of impending danger.

5. Courtship and establishment of territory.
6. Simple enjoyment, as one might play the piano or harmonica, just for the fun of it.

The present-day tendency is to decry the attribution of any human behavior to that of lower vertebrates. "Anthropomorphism," some call it. But the very word shows us how little people really know, for it is, I believe, a fact that the longer and more abstruse the word we use to describe a phenomenon, the less we know what we are talking about.

However that may be, I will, at the risk of being called an anthropomorphist, try, in the following pages, to describe some of my observations.

CHATTER

The best example of simple chatter among birds, in my experience, is that of a flock of feeding peep—least or semi-palmated sandpipers. Hidden in some nearby grass, I have often watched such a flock of peep scurrying hither and yon over freshly exposed flats. They keep up a constant twittering and calling, sometimes interspersed with a louder, higher-pitched complaint, as one, lazier and greedier than the other, tries to steal some tidbit from his neighbor. Occasionally, one of them will make a queer, trilling note like the bouncing of a xylophone hammer. The whole effect always reminds me of those times when, as a boy, I was sick in an upstairs bed while a tea party was going on below. Chatter, chatter, chatter.

I don't think the peep do it merely to keep contact, although this may be so. Certainly, as all at once they take wing, the chattering ceases. I rather think they do it as a sort of comfort to themselves. It makes each individual feel that he is part of a large flock, where there is safety in numbers—or at least where the mathematical chances of sudden disaster are much reduced. It is the single, fast-flying peep which utters the characteristic shrill note.

There are many other birds that have a tendency to chatter. Offhand, I think of crossbills, siskins, cedar waxwings, and English sparrows. They are, of course, all birds which gather in flocks. In fact, I have an idea that all those birds which habitually feed in flocks have the chattering tendency.

DISCUSSION OF PLANS

There comes a day in the fall when the beetlehead, or black-bellied plover, seem restless. The wind is very likely fresh from the northwest, and the air carries a distinct suggestion of winter. On such a day, the plaintive, musical call of these plover fills the marsh. Flocks of them, whistling loudly, will for no apparent reason rise up from a juicy-looking flat and then quickly settle down again.

"Going to move on," you say.

And you are quite right. Next morning there is hardly one left. Plenty of yellowlegs are about, and other shore birds, but no black-bellied plover.

Canada geese, I am pretty certain, communicate by voice. If one watches the actions of a flock, led by a big, white old gander, especially if they are looking over what appears to be unknown territory, one can hardly escape the conclusion that the leader is giving orders. There is, of course, no way of telling whether the honking which goes back and forth between them is actually a discussion of plans.

Certain it is, however, that the old gander may hold the flock high in the air, while he himself goes to investigate. I have seen this happen many times, and it seems inescapable that, when he is thoroughly satisfied, he calls them down by means of his voice.

Then again, it is interesting to watch a flock of geese, bound perhaps for the Carolinas, pass high above a flock feeding along our Cape Cod shores. Such a gabbling and a honking as then goes on!

"Don't be foolish," the migrating flock seems to say. "Come on south where it's warm."

"Mighty good eelgrass here," is the reply. "Why don't you come down and stay a while? You can go south later, if you want to."

Sometimes the high flock will waver, turn, and pitch down in. Sometimes the feeding flock will suddenly rise and follow along. More often, each flock will go its own way, and the noise will gradually subside.

But, of all the birds, crows appear to have the most complete system of communication, although, I must admit, I am far from being able to understand it. My son, Fred, and I have spent many hours trying to learn their language, without too much success. There is one series of rather soft "caws" which we feel sure is a "gather" call—that is, a call for the gathering of a small group or unit, not the mobilization of the entire crow population. It is usually uttered from some prominent place, like the roof of a house. Here eight or ten crows will convene. After a considerable period of cawing back and forth, one or two scouts are sent out to see where the best foraging for that day is to be had. Generally, in about fifteen minutes or

so, the scouts come back to report. Then there is a great
to-do, with all the crows talking at once. Apparently, however, they finally reach a decision, and one by one they fly
off, always in the same direction, and usually—if they can
be followed through the glasses—to the same spot. One day
it will be the Skiff Hill pastures, the next, the Beach Marsh,
and so on.

All this may sound rather fanciful, but, if one spends any
considerable amount of time with them, one can hardly escape the conclusion that some birds, at least, have a very
elaborate system of communication.

MAINTENANCE OF CONTACT

Here again, crows are perhaps the best example. They
appear to have definite outposts scattered over the country-
side, one within hearing distance of the other. Let the Big
Owl be found roosting in a pine tree, and the call goes out.
Crows can be seen flying toward the spot from every direction, until there is a black mob of them, calling, pitching,
badgering. At last the big brown bird becomes sick of the
din, and glides silently off to some more secure hiding place.

There seem to be degrees of mobilization. A stray cat
may call up only ten or fifteen crows, a red-tailed hawk
maybe twenty-five, while the Big Owl or a fox may bring
literally hundreds down on himself. Surely the outposts,
or liaison agents, must be able to indicate the severity of
the emergency and whether local or general mobilization
is indicated.

Of course, the commonest example of the use of bird
voices for contact is the constant calling during migration.
If one lies under the stars on the night of a big flight of

small birds, he will find the air filled with a continuous series of chips and chirps as the tiny folk traverse the dark heavens.

I have written in "Do-Nothing Day" of the peculiar grouping of one of these flocks. In the fall, one may see two or three bluebirds sitting on the peak of the barn roof. All around them in the cedars, on the ground, on the south platform of the house, are hundreds of chipping sparrows and pine warblers, with perhaps a prairie or some other warbler in addition. Suddenly the bluebirds begin their soft warble, and, after a few moments, fly off. Then there starts up a tremendous chipping and chirping. Soon the pine warblers take wing in ones and twos, followed more slowly by the sparrows, until finally the last straggler has gone and not a bird remains.

Obviously, this great, loose flock, which may take many minutes to get under way, keeps itself together by means of constant calling. And the flock seems to be led by bluebirds, sometimes aided by a robin or two.

WARNING OF IMPENDING DANGER

There can be no doubt that certain birds have calls which mean "Look out!" The sharp, explosive caws of the crow, usually in a series of four, are well known. The scream of the bluejay, sometimes of much annoyance to the hunter, is familiar to anyone who travels the woods. Nor is the significance of those calls limited to one species. The bluejay's scream, for instance, will alert not only all other birds within its range but all the animals as well.

Not so familiar is the alarm note of shore birds. I have never been quite able to attach any specific note to any specific species. I think the note, if heard by itself without all the attendant excitement, would readily identify the species. But as soon as it is uttered, there is a general turmoil. All the shore birds within hearing take wing. Large flocks of red-backed sandpipers hurtle into the air and sweep off in a body, twisting this way and that with perfect precision, now gleaming white, now suddenly turning dark.

Sometimes, one may pick up with the glasses the cause of all this disturbance. Perhaps it is the duck hawk, whose lightning turns always seem to be just a hair too late, or perhaps it is his smaller cousin, the merlin or pigeon hawk, or possibly one of those round-winged accipiters, the sharp-shinned or the Cooper's hawk.

For all of these, the shore bird's cry is the same. The note is shrill, high pitched, and insistent. Once you have heard it, there is no mistaking it. Not always, however, can you find the marauder. The sharpness of vision of these shore birds is unbelievable, and their ability to identify their enemies almost more astonishing. I have heard a red-backed sandpiper give the warning cry when the dangerous falcon was, to mere human eyes, only a tiny speck in the sky.

Very different is the effect produced by our friend, the marsh hawk, terrifying as he is to meadow larks and other grass-inhabiting birds. When the call goes out, it is much less emphatic. Only those shore birds which have chosen the tide holes or shut-in creeks take wing. Those on the open flats merely suspend their search for food for a moment, and cock a wary eye.

Occasionally, instead of flying when the alarm is given, a shore bird will "freeze." I have seen a beetlehead, when the cry came, lie on his belly on the mud and draw in his neck so that he looked like nothing more than a hunk of seaweed. Only his sharp eye, tilted up toward the sky, could give him away.

Perhaps all birds have a special call that means "Watch out! Danger!" Surely, many of them do. Whether one calls it bird language or not makes very little difference. There can be no question that when the call comes, most birds, and often certain animals, pay heed. And usually it is well for them that they do!

COURTSHIP AND ESTABLISHMENT OF TERRITORY

The theory that song is used by many birds to establish territorial boundaries during the nesting season seems reasonable and tends to be borne out by observation. It is, however, quite impossible to tell how much of the song can be attributed to this purpose and how much to a courtship performance. In many species, the males arrive first, and are followed at some later date by the females. For instance, this is particularly true of robins. If one discounts flocks of wintering robins, so often seen about these parts in February, the very red-breasted, dark-headed males arrive some weeks before the females. The male immediately starts trying to sing. His first attempts are often rather feeble, but after a few days his joyous song from a nearby oak every morning ushers in the sunrise.

This early song appears to be chiefly territorial in purpose, for let another male come too close, and a fight will ensue. Or, if the robin should catch sight of his reflection in a window pane, there may be a great to-do. But when his lady arrives, who shall say that his song is not aimed at her? Certainly, a robin in full song would melt a heart of stone.

Other bird performances seem to me much more definitely a courtship act. The scream of the red-shouldered hawk coming from high out of the air may represent a warning to other hawks, but his sudden, vertical plunge down to within a few feet of the treetops surely is done to impress his mate. The zooming boom of the night hawk, the flight performance of the woodcock, the drumming of the partridge, and the crow of the pheasant may serve both purposes, although I like to think of them as courtship activities.

To watch a pheasant crowing is quite an experience. He makes a mighty effort, and produces a horrible squawk. This is accompanied and followed by a brief but rapid drumming of his wings. If you listen closely, on a still day, you can hear the drumming sound coming immediately after the crow.

Another courtship act which fascinates me is that of the bittern. In the first place, one must admit that he is a funny-looking bird. He appears ludicrous when, in order to hide, he stands thin and straight with bill pointing toward the zenith. The light and dark stripes of his neck blend with the grass in which he is standing, and it takes a sharp eye

to pick him out. Most people are familiar with his "song," likened by some to the noise of the driving of a stake or the sucking of a pump. But it is much more than that. It has a rich, full-bodied quality as it comes booming out of a fresh-water marsh.

The bittern is so retiring that relatively few people ever see him perform. He goes through terrific contortions, as if he were becoming deathly ill, and then, suddenly, out comes the boom. Meanwhile, from somewhere at the base of his neck, where they usually remain safely hidden, appear two long, white plumes. For some time the bittern keeps up his pumping. Finally, perhaps from pure fatigue, he stops, and the white feathers vanish as mysteriously as they came.

Of recent years, we have had near the Farm House several pairs of nesting prairie horned larks. This tiny bird has a very insignificant song which I gather is not nearly as musical as that of his English cousin. However, he does his best. Up, up he flies, squeaking with all his might—higher and yet higher, until the eye, even with the aid of binoculars, can no longer follow without the help of a friendly white cloud. For a long while the squeaking goes on, until all at once the little bird plunges down to earth and lights close by the nest where his mate is sitting. Surely this, too, is a courtship performance.

Of all the bird songs, perhaps the crow's song is the most definitely an act of wooing. So shy is he, however, that few people have ever heard him perform. I have talked with experienced field ornithologists who had never heard the crow's song, and who, when I spoke of it, looked at me with disbelieving eyes. I myself have heard it only very rarely.

One day my cousin and I were lazily paddling down the Ipswich River. There came from downstream that curious, staccato note of the crow which resembles the rapid plucking of a taut string. Over and over he repeated it.

"Keep quiet," my cousin whispered. "Maybe he'll sing for us."

We drifted slowly downstream, making no motion and no sound. And then, just as we came around a bend, the crow began to sing. He and his ladylove were sitting near the top of a high pine and from his wide open beak were coming a series of clear, bell-like notes. Musical and sweet, they were as different from the crow's normal voice as anything could be. Suddenly the singer caught sight of us, and, with a series of protesting caws which seemed to contain a definite element of reproach, both crows flew off out of sight. Since then, only once have I heard the crow's love song.

As a practical matter, I suppose it makes little difference if bird song is territorial in nature, or whether it is definitely directed toward obtaining and holding a mate. Certain it is that bird song reaches its peak during the nesting season. Here in Massachusetts, this occurs late in May, after which the singing gradually peters out. Early July may bring about a slight recrudescence, but by the end of the month it has largely disappeared. Except for the indefatigable vireo, only an occasional whistle from an oriole, or a halfhearted attempt by a robin interrupts the sleepy buzz of August locusts.

SIMPLE ENJOYMENT

For some reason, it seems to be unfashionable to suppose that birds, or animals, for that matter, do anything just for the fun of it. I am sure, however, that frequently they do.

The hill and cedar bank, which separate the Farm House from the Nauset Marsh, face south. Come then, when there is a good fresh sou'wester blowing, and watch the herring gulls. They will start at the east end of the Cedar Bank, meet the updraft, and with not a single wingbeat slide up along the brow of the hill, headed due west. However, when they come to where the hill drops down to the Salt Pond Creek, instead of scaling off across the Salt Pond and so over to the Great Pond or perhaps the West Shore—as is often their custom—they make an abrupt turn to the east, coast off down to leeward, luff up over the east edge of the Cedar Bank and slide by again. I have watched a single gull repeat this performance eight or ten times, and I cannot escape the notion that, like so many humans, the gull enjoys the feeling of effortless travel.

When it comes to humor, I must say that I have never heard a bird laugh. There have been times when I was sure that black ducks were laughing at me up their sleeves—or up their wings—but I never actually heard one do it. The loon's mocking laugh is not of this world, and surely has nothing to do with humor. I have been told that tame crows sometimes laugh, but all I know for certain is that they, like many practical jokers, have a perverted sense of humor, and cunningly hide trinkets or bits of jewelry that have been left around the house.

As far as singing for the fun of it is concerned, I can't help thinking of the red-eyed vireo. He doesn't have what could be called a beautiful song. In fact it is so indefinite that one can listen to it for an hour or more without actually hearing it. Day in, day out, the incessantly repeated trio of notes goes on and on. It does not matter how hot or sultry the day, there is no minute of it when one cannot hear the vireo's song. Moreover, he keeps it up way through the summer when other birds have become silent. He reminds me of a young lad strolling down the street loudly whistling. And I am quite sure the boy and the bird are doing it because they just plain like the sound of it.

Of all the Eastham birds, the meadow lark seems to belong most particularly to the Farm House. With us, they are permanent residents, and in those rare years when there is long-standing snow on outer Cape Cod, many of them die. About 1939, for instance, the Cape had one snowstorm after another, and the meadow larks practically disappeared. But now they are more numerous than I have ever seen them. Last November we saw eighteen flying in a loose flock —more than I have ever before seen together.

But it is of the meadow lark's song that I particularly wish to speak. You may hear those clear, sweetly whistled notes in any month of the year—not so often in winter, perhaps, as in spring, but often enough to brighten the winter sky. Here is no question of maintaining territorial boundaries. Here is no question of nuptial activity. Surely the meadow lark is singing for the simple joy of it, and because he is, no doubt, proud of his achievement.

As I lie in bed on a cold, still December day, and wonder if I will ever have the courage to leave it, suddenly from the top of a nearby cedar come those few clear notes. They make me feel ashamed of my laziness, and I get up with a zest I would not otherwise have had. Perhaps, while the bacon is frying, even I break out into "song." And this I do, I can assure one and all, neither to keep off trespassers —a method which, incidentally, might prove effective—nor in order to impress my wife. I do it simply because I feel like it.

My guess is that birds sing for the same reason.

22. *The Big Owl*

O F ALL the bird sounds, perhaps the hooting of the
Big Owl—the great horned owl—is at once the most
thrilling and the most fearful. It has great carrying power
and seems loud when coming from afar, and yet, when it
arises from close by, it is as soft as the cooing of a mourning
dove. It has the quality of ventriloquism, and only with
great difficulty, if at all, can its source be definitely located.

I remember the first time I ever heard it. One foggy morning I was walking through a path which ran along a ridge
in the pitch pine forest northeast of the Farm House. Suddenly, from the next ridge, the sound came booming out:
"Whoo–Whahoo! Whoo! Who?" Prickles went up and
down my spine. I wasn't exactly afraid, but I glanced over
my shoulder, half expecting to see an Indian dodge behind
a tree. "Whoo–Whahoo! Whoo! Who?" it came again.
This time there could be no doubt. It was asking the same
old question.

I have heard that Grand Old Man of the River, the great

blue heron, in his croaky, sneezy way, ask it as he slowly flaps south through the night. I have heard the hermit thrush, in measured cadences, fill the dark pine woods with the same question. And I have heard the challenge of a flock of geese, as, high through a frosty sky, they spear their way toward sunnier climes. But, of them all, the most insistent voice is that of the Big Owl.

Possibly the owl was simply questioning my right to be there, for after I had crossed the next ridge, and dropped into the hollow beyond, I caught a glimpse of a ghostly, gray shadow drifting quietly out of sight through the trees. And shortly I discovered, near the top of one of the larger pines, the nest of sticks from which he or his mate had flown. It was late March, and I did not climb the tree to investigate further. I had read too many stories of the ferocity of such owls, especially when they have young in the nest.

Since then, I have heard the Big Owl many times in many places. Once, last summer, two of them crooned a duet from the meadow just below the Farm House. It was ten o'clock of a black, drizzly night in September when first we heard them. I went out in the dark, bare-headed, the better to listen. One was lower-pitched, and had a curious catch in the second syllable. (Horned owls usually, but not always, hoot in a series of five.) The other, following almost immediately after the first, was just a third of an octave higher. Also, it was softer in tone, and more coaxing. I wondered which was the husband and which the wife. One would have thought that the softer, higher-pitched voice belonged to the lady, but somehow I have an awful feeling that those low, booming notes were hers. If so, there could be little doubt who was the boss of that family.

It occurred to me to try squeaking like a mouse, an art at which I consider myself an expert, and one which will frequently attract nearby owls of any kind. The moment I began squeaking, both the owls stopped hooting. For a while, I kept on, and then I suddenly felt as if those great birds were floating by, right over my head. The night was black dark and I could barely make out the peak of the barn roof. All at once, the thought of my exposed and balding pate overwhelmed me, and I made for the house.

I sat silently by the fire for a few minutes. Sure enough, soon the duet began again. Was it my imagination, or was there in fact a more defiant quality to that low-pitched, vibrating hoot?

I do not know how common such a harmonized duet is among the horned owls. I have heard it once since, in a spot some hundred miles from the Farm House. In every respect, it was identical with the first performance, save that it occurred in late December, only a month or so before nesting activities usually begin.

You don't often get a good look at the Big Owl. He will drift off silently before you, a slightly lighter shadow against the darker shadow of the woods, and quickly disappear. Only owls have feathers so constructed that the wingbeat, be it ever so powerful, causes nary a sound. The Big Owl, apparently, can see perfectly well during the day, though he does most of his hunting by twilight, moonlight, or starlight. In this respect, he is unlike some smaller owls which, in daylight, may huddle quietly against a tree trunk and allow a close approach. I once was shown a tiny saw-whet owl, no bigger than your fist, sitting in a thick cedar at a distance of less than two feet. Not so the Big Owl. You are lucky if you startle him close by and he shows you his white neckpiece as, flying silently off, he twists his great round head to look down at you.

Once, and only once, I had a close view of him. We were sitting before a low fire, one evening in May, and were seriously considering lighting the lamps. Suddenly, a dark shape swooped down in front of the window and lit atop a small cedar not sixty feet away. We crept out the back door and peeked around the corner of the house. And there he was! He looked for all the world like a huge black cat, sitting there in the top of the little tree, his big head bent slightly forward and his cat's "ears" cocked, obviously looking to the meadow below for his supper. Again the prickles went up and down my spine. I was half glad, half sorry, when he finally slipped off the tree and disappeared into the gloom.

There are other "big" owls, of course. There is the snowy

owl, monarch of the beaches, whose fierce golden eye warns all and sundry to stay clear. And there is the barred owl, also a big owl, but by and large a friendly fellow who is likely to make his winter residence right in the middle of the city park. His seven-syllable hoot, with its sharply down inflected ending, has a gentler quality. I won't say that it doesn't have the eeriness which is peculiar to all owls, but it seems more down to earth and nearer home. And then there is the great gray owl, about which I know nothing. But to me, the great horned owl is the only Big Owl.

Not always do they hoot, or croon duets. Once we heard, my wife and I, a strange, high-pitched call. It suggested some bird in distress and we went to investigate. As we came nearer, we found it more and more difficult to tell whence the sound was coming. Consequently we separated, in order to try to bracket it. And then, as we converged, a big bird swept out of a small pine and sailed off into the forest. Was the Big Owl trying to entice some unwary bird into the range of his talons? Or, if not a bird, possibly some unscrupulous mammal bent on taking advantage of a creature in distress?

No, not always do they sing duets. Have you ever heard, in the dead of night, a searing, blood-curdling scream? A scream that jumps you out of your bunk with your hair on end? Be reassured. It's not a woman being foully murdered. It's the Big Owl, who has missed his pitch and allowed some dainty morsel, perhaps a skunk, to escape his clutch.

Many people hate the Big Owl.

"He's a bad actor," some say to me. "He takes a lot of ducks."

"Well, what if he does?" say I. "He has a taste for duck,

and so do I. But I bet he takes a lot more rats than either of us."

He takes crows, too, and while I happen to like crows (but not to eat), I know that they are not always welcome. Crows destroy duck eggs, and the Big Owl does more to control the crow population than does man with all his gadgets.

All this reminds me of a story my father used to tell. One day he was out in the brush, shooting partridge with a man we may call Mr. X. A kingfisher came by overhead and Mr. X. shot him.

"What in the world did you shoot that kingfisher for?" asked my father.

"Oh," said Mr. X. "Kingfishers destroy more trout than any other living thing."

A short time later the two hunters came upon a huge black snake which Mr. X. up and shot.

"For Heaven's sake!" cried my father. "What did you shoot *him* for?"

"Why, don't you know," replied Mr. X., "that black snakes destroy more kingfisher's eggs than any other living thing?"

The philosophy of those who are so keen on predator control often seems to me much the same as Mr. X.'s. I would think it far better to see to it that abundant feeding and nesting areas be provided, and to let the owls and crows fight it out between themselves.

Come, some night ir February, and stand for a while in the tall wood. There is no sound other than the rustle of a light breeze through a few tenacious oak leaves. Overhead, a scattering of bright stars twinkles through the branches in a vain attempt to pierce the gloom of the forest. And then from a distance comes that vibrating, awe-inspiring call. Nearer and nearer it approaches, until at last it seems to fill all surrounding space. Soft, yet queerly penetrating, it reaches into your soul.

As the sound dies away in the distance, there comes from afar the muted whistle of a locomotive. Strangely, it seems to have captured a trace of the eternity in the Big Owl's voice.

"Whoo–Whahoo! Whoo! Whoooo!" goes the train.

And "Whoo-Whahoo! Whoo! Who?" repeats the owl.

Dare you answer?

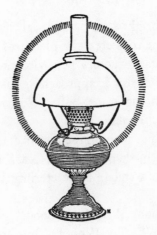

23. Bed Time

THE day is done. The supper things have all been washed and put away. The kerosene lamp on the dining table gives off a soft yellow glow that highlights the geese on the walls, and leaves deep shadows in the corners. In the fireplace, an oak fire is quietly burning, which, together with the lamp, radiates enough heat to keep the low-ceilinged living room reasonably warm.

We sit by the fire and talk tonight about nothing very serious. We feel comfortably tired after our exertions of the day, comfortably fed, and comfortably warm. The mantel clock ticks quietly on, and suddenly strikes ten in its characteristically erratic way.

First one person and then another yawns, stretches and departs for bed, until at last only the Old Man himself is left. Finally even he gets up from his chair, takes his last weather observation, checks up on the kitchen stove, and puts out the lamps. Being the last to go, he can enjoy the luxury of leisurely undressing before the warmth of the dying fire. By slowly turning around and around, he thoroughly toasts himself. At last, however, he can procrastinate no longer. He puts up the fire screen, dashes rapidly into his bedroom, and takes the desperate plunge between the ice-cold sheets.

Through the open living-room door, he can see dancing lights and shadows and hear quiet sounds as the fire burns down. From the pantry comes a barely audible scratching, indicating that the pantry mouse is busily engaged in finding himself some supper. Outside, there is a slight rustling, as the light breeze stirs the cedars, while the sudden barking of a dog suggests that Mr. Fox is bothering someone's chickens.

Rest now, little Farm House. Your flock is safely in bed and sound asleep. Thank you for the wonderfully good times you have given us.

Good night.